LEARN FROM THE LEGENDS:
BLUES KEYBOARD

Great Licks and Interviews with the Stars

ISBN 0-7390-0953-2 Book
ISBN 0-7390-0961-3 Book and CD
ISBN 0-7390-0962-1 CD

Cover photo: Karen Miller

Performers on the CD:
Karen Ann Krieger, *piano*
Brian Fullen, *drums*
Peter Huttlinger, *guitar*
Jeff Cox, *bass*

KAREN ANN KRIEGER
& STEPHAN FOUST

Table of Contents

Introduction

The blues as we know it is a century old and counting. Its roots spring from the African-American experience, but its branches now include the contributions of numerous white Americans and several British artists.

Some blues purists believe you can't play the music if you haven't lived it. Others hold that it's not important how you live, but what you feel.

Regardless of where you personally stand on that debate, one fact is certain: your ability to play the blues or any of its related idioms will be enhanced with a clearer understanding and knowledge of exactly what's happening musically.

A significant amount of today's popular music is, at its core, blues-based. Chuck Leavell, Reese Wynans, Dr. John and Al Kooper, the four legendary performers profiled in this book, know this well—-they have, in fact, been at the heart of this blues revival since the 1960s and will likely continue to be well into the new millennium.

In this book, these four artists will tell you about their early years and musical beginnings.

You'll see and hear music in each of their styles so that you can practice on your own piano.

You'll also pick up licks and registrations for the classic Hammond B-3 organ, still the instrument of choice for many of today's finest rock and blues players.

Be advised that a basic level of technical skill is needed to play the exercises in this book. Likewise, the ability to read music will be helpful; however, a chapter of basic theory is included as a reference, if you need some review.

For simplicity, all musical licks are written in the keys of C major or C minor, then transposed to a second key. In addition, each chapter contains several complete blues pieces that are not transposed.

Utilized to its fullest, this book will serve as a springboard for you to develop your own style of blues playing. Check out the available CD, then play these licks and make them your own.

Improvisation can be a statement, a way to honestly express your own unique feelings. Through the blues, you can communicate in ways you may have never dreamed possible. Your initial curiosity today may lead to a lifetime commitment tomorrow.

The great Al Kooper once put it this way: "Like my heroes, Muddy Waters, B.B. King and Ray Charles, I will play the blues until my hands can't move anymore."

The tradition lives on generation after generation. Listen, learn...and become a part of it.

Karen Ann Krieger and Stephan Foust

Acknowledgments

This is the second in a series of *Learn From the Legends* instructional books. Once again, we have truly been blessed in having had the assistance, support and friendship of numerous gifted people throughout this project. These pages are a tribute to their energy, effort and enthusiasm.

Our special appreciation goes to everyone at Alfred Publishing Company, a talented team that shares our vision for this instructional series.

We thank Ron Manus, Link Harnsberger, Bruce Goldes, Dian Buchman, Brad Davis, Rose Lane Leavell, Pamela Sullivan, Peter Himberger, Elizabeth Cormier, Stacey Fountain, Jack Pearson, Buck Williams, Dennis Charles, Sylvia Miller, Sue Ann Reinisch, Robert Morsch, Todd Allen Sanders, Michael Kramer, Kevin Litwin, Paul Zonn, and Jimmy and Karen Hall.

We remember and recognize Edward and Josephine Krieger, Lyman and Margaret Foust, and Cassius and Margaret Ellen Richardson for embodying us with the spirit of teaching and a love for learning.

We offer our gratitude to Gregg Allman for keeping us pointed in the right direction.

Our applause goes to the talented musicians who believed in the project and found the groove in the recording session at Nashville's Mainframe Studio: Brian Fullen, drums and producer; Peter Huttlinger, guitar; Jeff Cox, bass; Nathan Smith, engineering and mastering.

Most significantly, we aim the spotlight center stage on Chuck Leavell, Reese Wynans, Mac "Dr. John" Rebennack and Al Kooper—legends, all. Take a bow, guys. Your desire to pass on your lifetime of knowledge, combined with your willingness to share your astounding skills, is an inspiration.

May the blues live forever!

Karen Ann Krieger and Stephan Foust

About the Recording

An optional CD is available for this book. The track numbers on the CD correspond with the track numbers listed throughout the book: Track #

When more than one example is recorded on a single track, it will be designated by a decimal following the track number: (1.1, 1.2, etc.)

The recotding has been mixed with the piano on one channel that can be dialed out so you can play along with the band.

Tuning   Track I

This track will allow you to tune your electronic keyboard to the CD.

Section 1
Basic Music Theory & Keyboard Technique

For those with a background in music theory, feel free to skip this chapter. However, if you feel like you need a review, or perhaps feel you'll benefit from another perspective, take a look.

If you're new to the world of music theory, memorize and process the following information. It will help you understand how it all works at the keyboard. This knowledge will also make it easier for you to communicate with other musicians.

Reading Music

Many keyboard players play blues and rock 'n' roll by ear, but why not try to develop your eyes, too? You can become a better reader if you take notice of intervals—the distance between notes.

Play through and study the examples below. If you need more practice, turn to your favorite licks. Then, before you begin to play them, read the intervals and name the notes.

Rhythm

Everyday life has a pulse: a baby's beating heart, a child skipping rope, downtown traffic. In music, that pulse is organized into *measures* which group combinations of notes and rests to create rhythm.

The number of beats in each measure is indicated by the *time signature*. The top number tells you the number of beats in each measure. The bottom number tells you what kind of note gets one beat.

For example: **4** = 4 beats per measure
4 = quarter note gets one beat

6 = 6 beats per measure
8 = eighth note gets one beat

If you are faced with a complex rhythm, try *tapping* it out before playing the notes, just like a percussion player. Your success rate will be much greater. *Counting out loud* as you play can help, too.

Study the rhythms below before you tackle the licks in the book.

Note Relationships

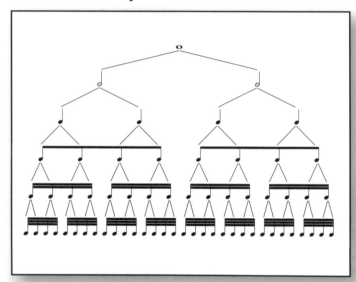

Rest Relationships

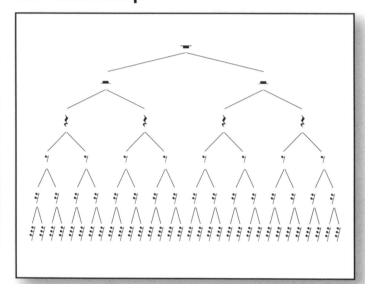

Dotted Notes

A dot after a note increases its length by one half of its original value.

$\textrm{d.}$ = $\textrm{d}\smile\textrm{d}$ = 3 beats

$\textrm{d.}$ = $\textrm{d}\smile\textrm{d}$ = 1½ beats

$\textrm{♪.}$ = $\textrm{♪}\smile\textrm{♪}$ = ¾ beats

Triplets

When 3 notes are grouped together with a figure "3" above or below the notes, the group is called a Triplet.

The 3 notes are played in the time of 2 notes of the same value.

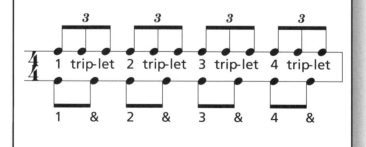

Major 5-Finger Positions and Major Chords

The ability to play the first five steps in all scales, hands together, will help you get ahead of the game. These 5-finger positions are the quickest way to learn basic rock 'n' roll chords while developing your keyboard technique. The best way to learn these chords is to memorize the patterns. The following formulas will help you find the correct keys.

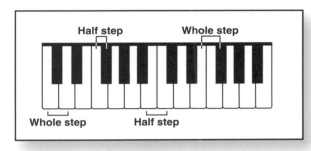

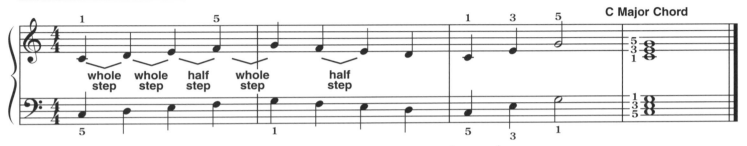

For major 5-finger positions follow the pattern:
whole step, whole step, half step, whole step.

For major chords play:
the **1st**, **3rd** and **5th** notes of the major position.

Each major position has a certain arrangement of five piano keys. The keyboards below give a visual picture of these keys. The positions are grouped according to their color (black and white). Notice their similarity: C and G are all white; D and A have one black key in the middle; D♭ and A♭ are opposites of D and A; etc. Play and memorize the following 5-finger positions and major chords. Follow the example above.

Major 5-Finger Positions Chart

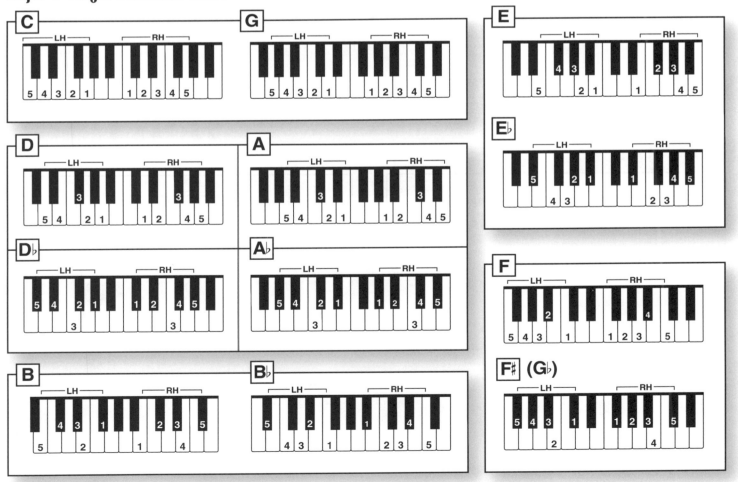

Minor 5-Finger Positions and Minor Chords

If you've learned and memorized the 12 major 5-finger positions and major chords, the hard work is over. To play the minor 5-finger positions and chords, put your hand in the major position, then move your middle finger down one half step. Fingers 1-2-4-5 will remain over the same keys.

The downward movement of the 3rd finger puts you in the minor position. Play 1-3-5 for a minor chord.

If you get lost, you can always find a minor 5-finger position and minor chord using the steps below.

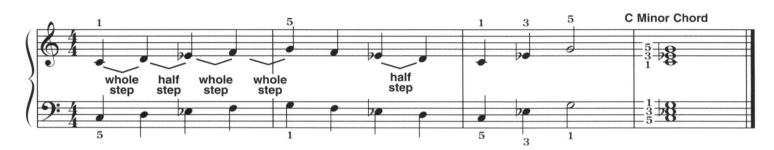

To play minor 5-finger positions follow this pattern:
whole step, half step, whole step, whole step.

To find minor chords, play:
the **1st**, **3rd** and **5th** notes of the minor 5-finger position.

Minor 5-Finger Positions Chart

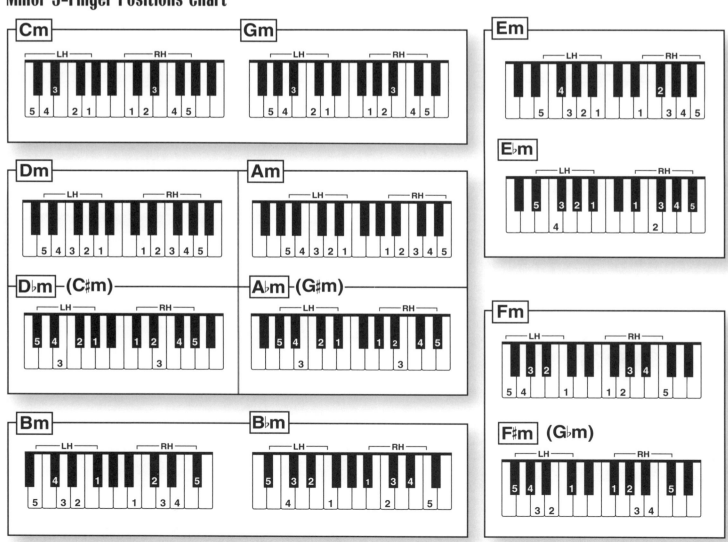

More About Chords

You'll find the chords in this book contain both basic and more advanced chords. The ability to identify them will help you apply these chords to your own licks. Here's how it works:

Each of the seven scale degrees can be the *root* of a chord. The root is the lowest note and the name of the chord.

The chords on the I, IV and V scale degrees are the most-played chords in rock 'n' roll. Learn to play the I, IV and V chords in all 12 major and 12 minor keys.

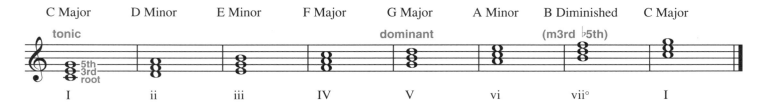

Chord Inversions

Every major and minor chord has two *inversions*.

Inversions rearrange chord tones so that either the third or the fifth becomes the lowest bass note.

In music notation, there are different ways of writing chord inversions.

This musical shorthand was popular in the 17th–18th centuries. It was based on intervals.

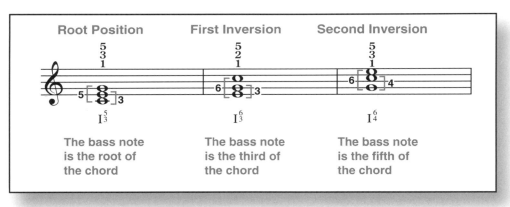

In pop and rock music, another system is used. Sometimes a chord's letter name is paired with a slash mark. The letter that follows the slash tells you what note should be the lowest note—the bass note. This, too, creates chord inversions.

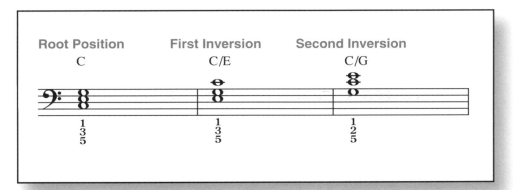

Left-Hand Chord Inversion Exercises

The following chord inversion exercises are a good way to develop your technique.

Try hands alone and hands together. Then play inversions in other keys.
You'll be able to play the enclosed licks more easily with this skill.

Right-Hand Chord Inversion Exercises

Seventh Chords

Seventh chords are very popular in rock 'n' roll. They're easy to learn if you already know your major and minor chords.

You can make any root position chord into a seventh chord by adding one more note a third above the top note.

Seventh chords look like a stack of four pancakes, either all lines or all spaces. The lowest pancake is the name of the chord.

There are five basic kinds of seventh chords. Each has its own special mix of 3rds and 7ths:

- C major seventh (Cmaj^7) — major third and major seventh, (C-E-G-B).
- C seventh (C^7 dominant seventh) — major third and minor seventh, (C-E-G-B♭).
- C minor seventh (Cm^7) — minor third and minor seventh, (C-E♭-G-B♭).
- C half-diminished seventh (Cm$^{7(♭5)}$ or C^{ø7}) — minor third, diminished fifth, minor seventh, (C-E♭-G♭-B♭).
- C diminished seventh (C$^{°7}$) — minor third, diminished fifth, diminished seventh, (C-E♭-G♭-B♭♭).

Seventh Chords on the Keyboard

Seventh chords are easy to find on the keyboard.

First visualize, then feel the major seventh one half step below the root's octave.

Visualize, then feel the minor seventh one whole step below the root's octave. The diminished seventh will be a step and a half below the root's octave.

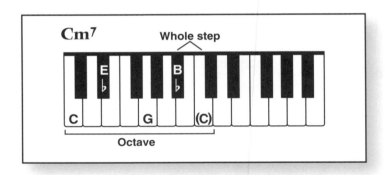

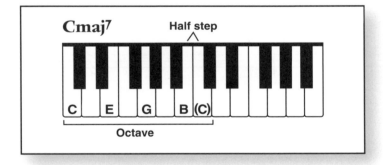

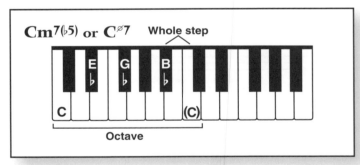

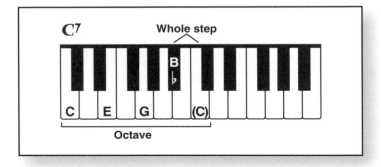

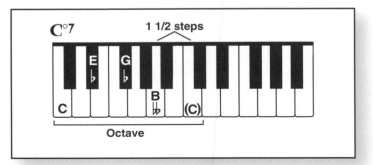

Seventh Chord Inversion Exercises

The following exercises will help you develop your blues piano skills. Start slowly and gradually increase your tempo.

Key Signatures and Major Keys

Sharps or flats that immediately follow the clef signs are called *key signatures*. Key signatures tell us what notes are to be played sharp or flat throughout the piece.

Sharps in a key signature always appear in the following order:

F#, C#, G#, D#, A#, E#, B#

In a sharp key signature, the key note is one half step above the last sharp. For example, if your key signature has two sharps (F#, C#), the piece will use the notes of the D major scale. The D scale is spelled D-E-F#-G-A-B-C#-D.

Flats in a key signature always appear in the following order:

B♭, E♭, A♭, D♭, G♭, C♭, F♭

In a flat key signature, the key note is the next-to-last flat. For example, if your key signature has two flats (B♭, E♭), B♭ is the next-to-last flat. Your piece will use the notes of the B♭ scale. The B♭ scale is spelled B♭-C-D-E♭-F-G-A-B♭.

Two exceptions are the keys of C and F. The key of C has no sharps or flats. The key of F has one flat, B♭.

Key Signatures and Relative Minor Keys

All minor scales share a key signature with a major scale. They're "related" because they have the same key signature. The name of the relative minor key can be found by counting down three half steps from the name of the major key.

For example: to find the relative minor key of C, count down three half steps to A. Therefore, C major and A minor have the same key signature: no sharps or flats. Using the key signature of the major scale creates the *natural minor scale*. The A *natural minor scale* is spelled A-B-C-D-E-F-G-A.

Another example: The key of C minor has E♭'s key signature, three flats. It follows that the C natural minor scale is spelled C-D-E♭-F-G-A♭-B♭-C.

Circle of 5ths

The circle of 5ths dates back several centuries to Germany. It's still a useful musical tool today. It visually helps you to learn key signatures and the notes in every major scale.

The circle arranges all 12 keys by the interval of a 5th. If you move clockwise from C, you'll notice the number of sharps in a key increases, too.

For example, the key of C has zero sharps or flats. Moving clockwise up a 5th, you'll see that the key of G has one sharp, F#. D has two, F#, C#, etc.

If you move counterclockwise, the number of flats increases. For example, the key of F has one flat, B♭. The key of B♭ has two, B♭ and E♭.

Try to memorize the circle of 5ths.

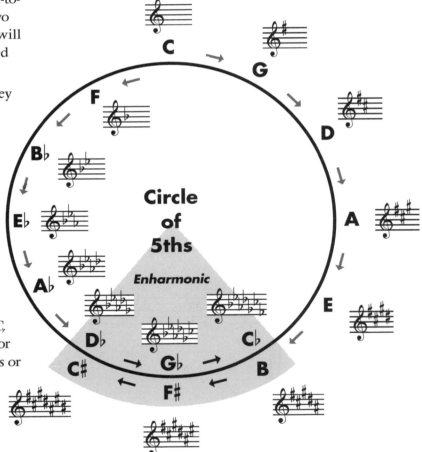

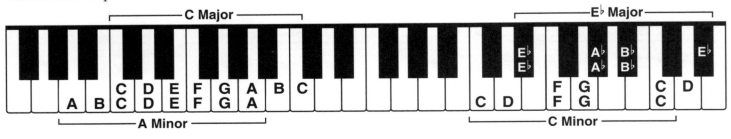

Major Scale Practice

Practice and memorize these major scales until they are easy to play. Scale technique will help you play the enclosed licks. Practice all scales hands alone and then hands together.

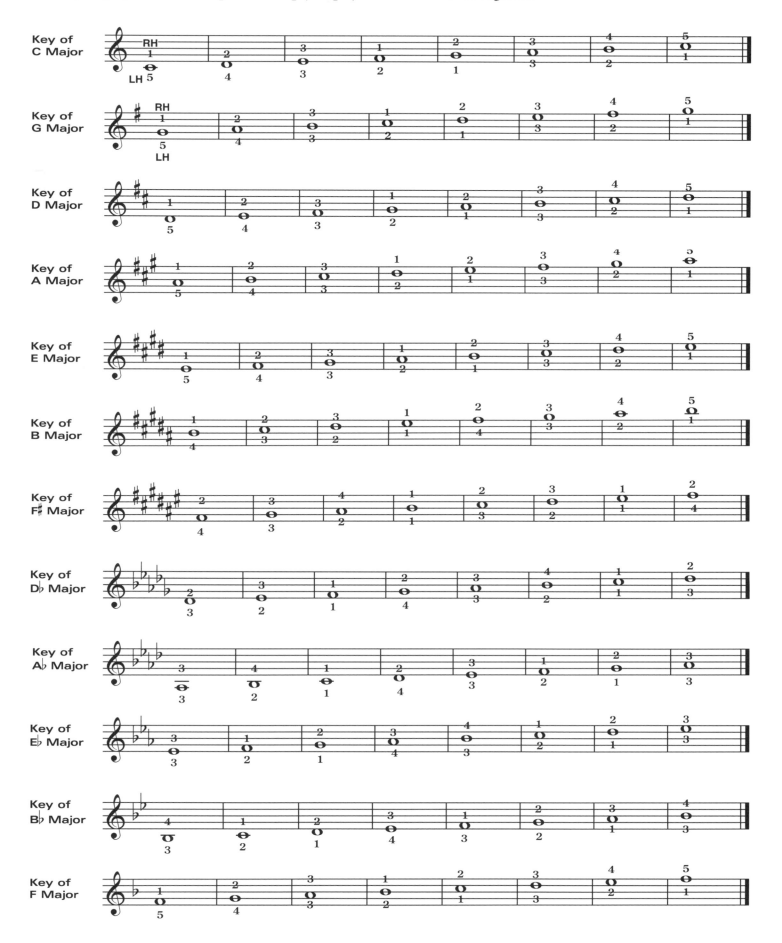

The Basic 12-Bar Blues Progression

To play the blues, a solid foundation and understanding of theory is necessary. Play, memorize and transpose these chords to your favorite blues keys.

The Blues Scale

The blues scale consists of the following intervals: m3, P4, ♭5, P5, m7.
For a better understanding of intervals, see theory page 5.
Play and memorize the blues study below. Try both fingerings to see which works best for you.

C Blues Scale

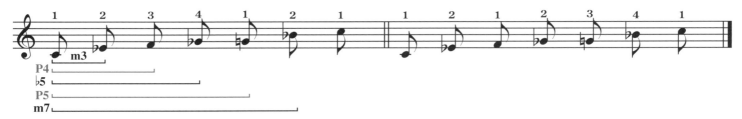

To see the blues scale in every key, turn to page 96.

C 12-Bar Blues   Track 4

On the recording, this example is played three times. The first time is as written, the second and third times eliminates the right hand to allow you to improvise freely using the C blues scale.

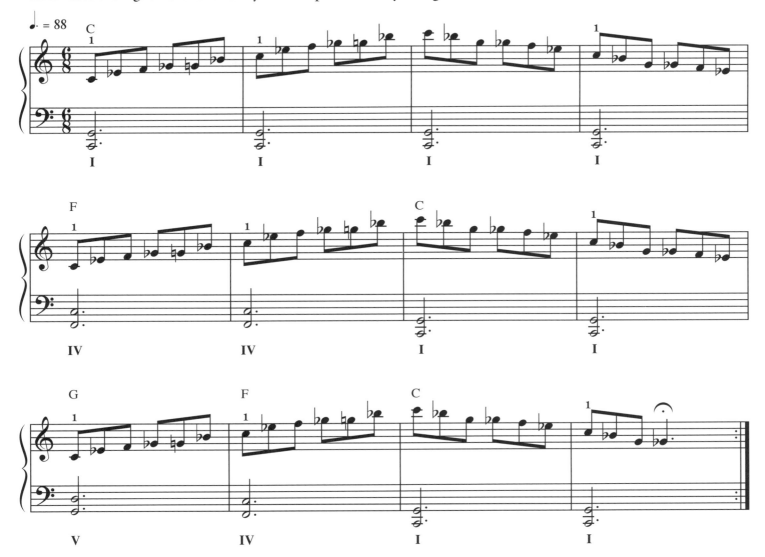

For more practice, improvise with tracks 2 and 3 (p. 16) using the C and G blues scales.

Section 2
Chuck Leavell

His musical resume reads like a tour of the Rock and Roll Hall of Fame: *The Allman Brothers, The Rolling Stones, Eric Clapton, Aretha Franklin, George Harrison,* to name just a few. He's played with them all and influenced them all. But even while he's left his mark on the music of these legendary groups and solo artists, they've also left their mark on him. Alabama native Chuck Leavell is, and always has been, a quick study, open-minded and eager to learn.

"My mother played piano and that's really how I learned," Chuck remembers. "My mom could play adequately and when I was young—five or six or so—she was my entertainment. I'd ask her to play something and she would stop whatever she was doing and sit down. I don't think she ever refused."

Standard tunes like "Spinning Song" or "Black Hawk Waltz" filled the house during the 1950s and fueled little Chuck's excitement. "I just loved it. It was a thrill for me. I would climb up on the stool and try to pick out some of the melodies. I couldn't learn sophisticated things, but my mother would play some simple piece and I would just play with it. That's what gave me a love for music."

And that love grew like a sapling. By the age of seven, Chuck was taking lessons with a local

Chuck Leavell with the Rolling Stones
From left: Keith Richard, Chuck Leavell, Charlie Watts, Ronnie Wood and Mick Jagger
Photo: from the collection of Chuck Leavell

Birmingham teacher. But the roots hadn't grown deep yet. "I loved playing, but my ears were far ahead of my eyes. I didn't want to read music and I just got lazy. That was my problem."

Still, he didn't entirely quit playing. Wedging it in between baseball games with the neighborhood boys, Chuck was still drawn to the keyboard. "I kept piddling around," he recalls. "I always kept the love for the instrument."

And for music itself. As the 1950s became the 1960s, the South was a hotbed of cultural and musical change. Chuck absorbed it all. "You grow up in the South, you can't help but hear so many great kinds of music—everything from gospel on Sunday mornings, to country music, to rhythm and blues. There was also folk music on TV and, of course, the British invasion was big at the time."

It was an eclectic and enriching mix. "My sister, Judy, and I listened to *Chad and Jeremy* and *The Kingston Trio;* then later, *The Beatles* and *Bob Dylan.* Dylan was just getting big and from listening to him, I learned some songs and some chords on an acoustic guitar."

It was only a matter of time until Chuck and some of those neighborhood boys traded the ball field for the band stage. At age 13, Chuck formed a band called *The Misfitz.* "We thought it was quite cool to have a 'z' at the end," he smiles. "And we did become pretty popular.

We played at school dances, then we landed a steady job at the Tuscaloosa YMCA. We played every Friday night and made ten bucks each. Eventually, we got a raise to twelve-fifty."

Not quite the big-time, but the guys were, in fact, good enough to be noticed by local television. Soon, they were also playing cover tunes on *Tuscaloosa Bandstand*. "There were four of us in the band then. It was a live show and they would have these placards made up that said things like 'Go get 'em, Chuck!' when I was playing a solo. It was so silly and corny, but it was a lot of fun and we enjoyed it."

Such success spurred Chuck to learn and play even more. When the junior high school band instructors came into class and demonstrated the various instruments, Chuck took the bait. "I wound up playing tuba in the school band for two years," Chuck smiles. "That experience gave me a sense of ensemble and working together, plus some sense of competition because we would all compete for first chair. I also began to hear when people were out of tune or were late. Those things all had a positive effect on me."

So when the guys in The Misfitz all went their separate ways, 15-year-old Chuck made up his mind to seek out new and better musicians. He didn't have to travel far. The world-famous *Muscle Shoals Sound Studio* was right up the road on the Jackson Highway. "What a great breeding ground that was," Chuck marvels. "Everyone from *Leon Russell* to Dylan to The Stones to Aretha Franklin and many, many more recorded there. Muscle Shoals just had a magic vibe about it and it was great to get involved."

And that involvement increased quickly. Chuck's growing keyboard skills were soon in demand and brought him much attention. "By the ripe old age of 17, I was having all sorts of musical experiences with different southern bands, plus lots of rhythm and blues sessions that paid me 15 bucks a song."

But even more importantly, the exposure to quality musicians and different styles was paying Chuck big dividends. He was learning at an incredible rate and opening his mind to new dreams. "I began to think about music in a different way. I went with my sister to a *Ray Charles* concert and *Billy Preston* was in the band. What I heard and saw that night had a profound effect. 'This is good,' I thought. 'I like this.' I made up my mind that that's what I wanted to do. I wanted to play in a band like that. I wanted to make music my career."

But as positive as it was to have a definitive goal, there was also a big downside. "I got to my senior year in high school and I received an offer to work at a studio in Birmingham. I transferred up there and went to work. Some guys and I also had a band together called *Care*. We played a lot of dates and I missed a lot of school."

Not surprisingly, that didn't sit too well with either school officials or Chuck's parents. Chuck had maintained a "B" average, but his absences were exceeding the legal limit. He was given a choice: give up the band or give up school. "I gave up school," Chuck admits. "That was a very tough thing for my parents to swallow, but both of them accepted it and supported my decision. It meant a lot to me."

At the time, of course, no one could be sure how it would all turn out. Dropping out was a huge gamble, and one that meets with failure most of the time. Still, Chuck decided to buck the odds because he desperately wanted a lifetime career as a professional musician, learning from and playing with the very best. Leaving school, he reasoned, didn't mean his education was over.

Chuck threw himself into the task of being successful. He continued gigging with his band, Care, and working at the studio. He made valuable contacts everyday—people who would soon heavily influence the direction of his life.

Keyboardist *Paul Hornsby* was one of them. "I had seen him play with *Duane and Gregg Allman* as part of *The Hourglass*," Chuck remembers. "I was honored to be working with him. Paul thought it was cool to play in a group with two keyboards, like he did with Gregg. He had this cut-down Hammond B-3 and he taught me all sorts of things, including a lot of Ray Charles licks. He also encouraged me to sing, which was another big plus."

Chuck Leavell and Karen Ann Krieger

Paul soon had another opportunity. Big things were happening in little Macon, Georgia, and Paul was on his way. "This was the early days of *Capricorn Records*, and *The Allman Brothers* had just been signed. The studio needed a staff band. Paul was invited to be the keyboard player and to get involved in producing."

Great for Paul, but just the opposite for Chuck—at least at first. He had lost his compass. "Here I had dropped out of school and all. I was feeling down and wondering what I was gonna do. So I decided I better get over to Macon and see for myself what it was all about."

What it was about would take Chuck to places he'd only dreamed.

With Paul's help and encouragement, Chuck joined a band called *Sundown*. The group cut an album, reorganized, then emerged again as the back-up band to Capricorn recording artist *Alex Taylor*—singer-songwriter *James Taylor's* older brother. "That was my first experience traveling across the United States playing clubs. We did it in a station wagon and a van. We played places such as *The Gaslight* in New York City and *The Whiskey A-Go-Go* in Los Angeles. We did college dates. We traveled north into Canada and south into Florida. We hit just about every state over the next two years. It was eye opening for a kid of 17."

Chuck himself was also opening some eyes. In between all the road work, Capricorn was using Chuck more and more in the studio. Well-known southern boogie bands like *Cowboy* were the early beneficiaries of Chuck's crisp playing.

Capricorn founder *Phil Walden* then hooked Chuck and the rest of Sundown up with one of the label's newly signed artists, the soon-to-be national treasure, *Mac Rebennack*, then best known as *Dr. John the Night Tripper*. "Mac didn't have a band at the time," Chuck recalls, "so they had us audition for him. We got the job and went out on the road. The rest is what I call my college education—or as Mac would say, my 'edumacation.'"

Dr. John had already hit the charts with his solo recording of "Right Place, Wrong Time," but as catchy as it was, the tune scarcely hinted at the depth of his knowledge. A night playing with the good doctor literally meant tripping through the rich musical heritage of New Orleans in all its styles: Creole, ragtime, funk, jazz,

dixieland, barrelhouse, boogie-woogie, gospel, spirituals, street marches and, of course, the blues. "I consider him a mentor," Chuck reflects. "And I consider him a friend."

In addition to all the different styles, the time with Dr. John also gave Chuck the chance to hone his chops on the organ. "Ninety percent of the time, Mac played the piano, so I played B-3. We had a pretty jam-up band. I was real pleased with it and I learned a lot—most of it backstage and during rehearsals, when I could sit and watch him and listen to those voicings."

In less than a year, however, Dr. John had moved on to another label, and the band was again without an artist. A disappointed Chuck was temporarily unemployed and understandably uncomfortable, but he needn't have worried. His life was about to change forever. "I went back to Tuscaloosa to see my folks and decide what the heck I was going to do. Then, I got a call from *Johnny Sandlin* at Capricorn."

Sandlin was producing what was planned to be Gregg Allman's first solo album. After Chuck came on board, things changed radically. "The entire Allman Brothers Band showed up and started jamming. I was a little confused. I was being employed to do one thing, when, in fact, something else was happening."

And what was happening made music history in 1972. The great slide guitarist Duane Allman had died the previous year, the victim of a tragic motorcycle accident. Seeking to redefine themselves, the remaining members of the group found their new sound with Chuck. Instead of replacing Duane with a second guitarist, they decided to add a second keyboardist. "After two weeks of these jam sessions, it all began to take shape," Chuck remembers. "The guys approached me and asked me if I'd be interested in joining. I thought about it for about a half a second and said 'yes.'"

Years of work and total commitment to a goal boiled down to a decision made in less than the tick of a clock. Chuck's impact on the band was immediate and profound. The Allman Brothers Band was already well on its way to a Rock and Roll Hall of Fame career; but, with the addition of Chuck, the guitar-based rock and blues band successfully refined and redefined its sound. Some of the recordings from the sessions did, in fact, become Gregg's first solo album, the seminal *Laid Back*. Other tracks became the Allmans' *Brothers and Sisters* album, the group's first to hit number one on the charts. "The interaction was so abundant," Chuck notes. "That was great music for me and probably some of the strongest I'll ever do."

But the great music has continued non-stop ever since. Chuck recorded two more albums with The Allman Brothers, remaining with the group until their highly publicized breakup in 1976. He then wasted no time forming the critically acclaimed jazz/rock/blues group *Sea Level*, with fellow Allman Brothers members *Jaimoe* on drums and *Lamar Williams* on bass. After five noteworthy albums, the group disbanded in 1982, and Chuck was quickly snatched up by The Rolling Stones as keyboardist-vocalist. He's been recording and touring with The Stones ever since and has also found frequent time to do the same with blues/rock guitar giant Eric Clapton, including a featured role on the 1992 Grammy Award-winning *Unplugged* album. Chuck remains a

much sought-after session player with dozens of credits to his name; and, as if that weren't enough to keep him busy, he recently accomplished a long-time goal with the solo release of *What's In That Bag?*, a Christmas album of family favorites.

Chuck is also someone who believes a person is never too old to learn something entirely new. Several years ago, he branched out into another area of interest: tree farming. *Charlane Plantation*, located southeast of Macon, is where Chuck calls home, and where he finds refuge from his grueling recording and touring schedule. This award-winning musician is also a multi-award-winning conservationist with a national reputation.

Despite all the accomplishments, Chuck remains surprisingly unaffected by it all. The history of rock and blues is filled with stories of people who couldn't deal with the pressure or the distractions. Chuck believes he has an answer. "I don't take any of it seriously," he laughs. "When I was with the Allmans, Jaimoe pulled me aside and said, 'You know, some cats are gonna be rock stars and some cats are gonna be musicians. Which do you want to be?'"

Chuck Leavell in concert.
Photo: Paul Natkin

It's a question worth proper pause and consideration—but with Chuck, there's no hesitation. "I'd play," he states emphatically, "whether I made a living at it or not. My motivation is the joy I get from it. That's been my attitude ever since my mother played for me as a kid."

And as any good tree farmer can tell you, a sapling will grow straight and tall when its roots are deep and strong.

Review this page to understand the "Chuck Leavell style."

Licks in the Style of Chuck Leavell

For a more bluesy sound, feel in four and stress/lean on beats 2 and 4.

DRY BRANCH BLUES Track 6

"Add slides, grace notes wherever possible."—C.L.

Track 7.1

7a.

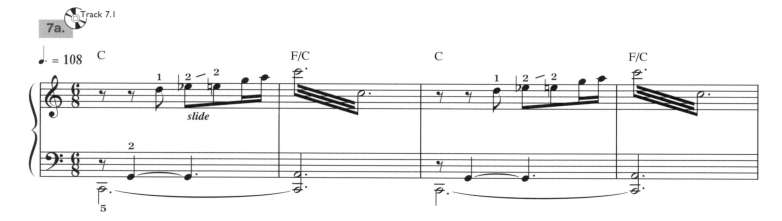

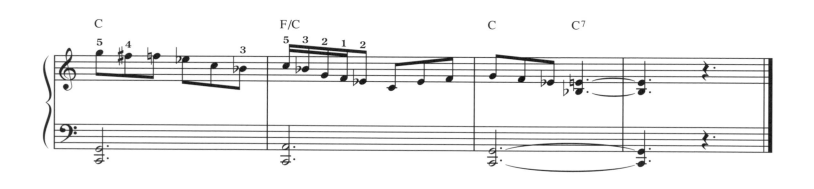

Track 7.2

7b.

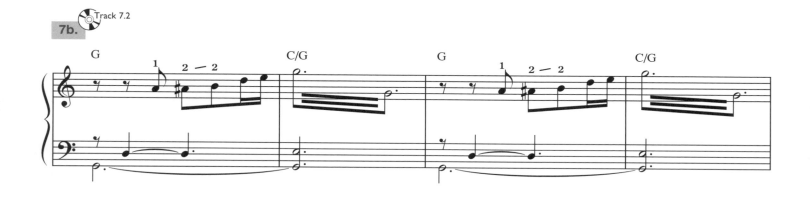

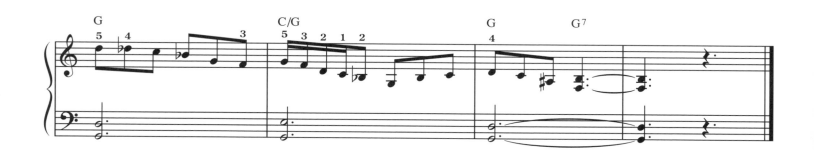

8a. Track 8.1

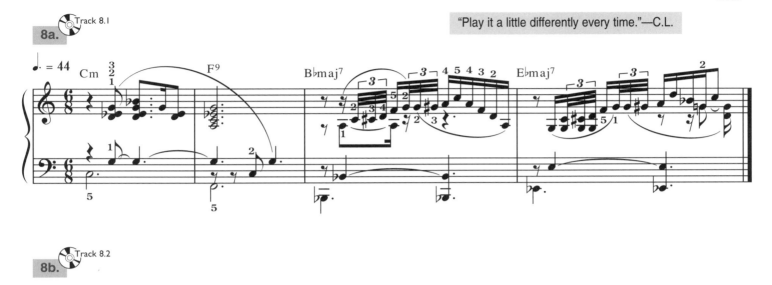

8b. Track 8.2

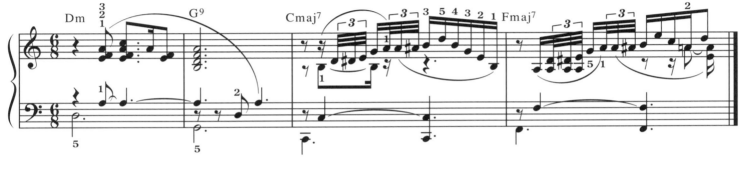

On Physical Conditioning . . .

9a. Track 8.3

"If I have a tour or a recording coming up, I'll prepare by spending a couple hours a day doing stretching exercises. I'll also run and work out. It's very important to be aware of your body and avoid physical problems."—C.L.

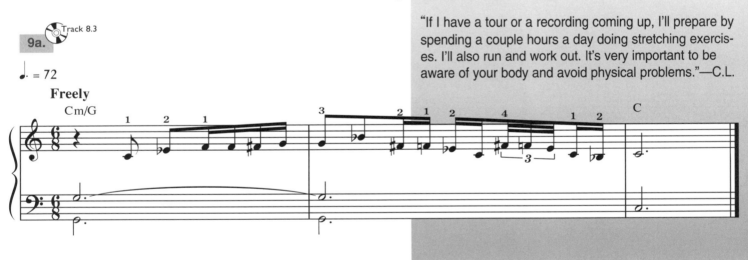

9b. Track 8.4

Track 9.1   For a more bluesy sound, lean on beats 2 and four.

10a.

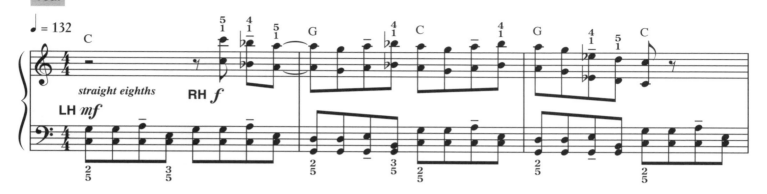

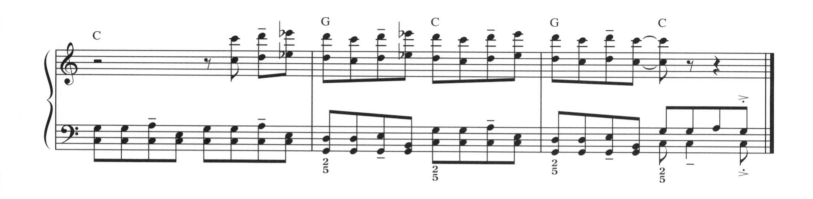

Track 9.2

10b.

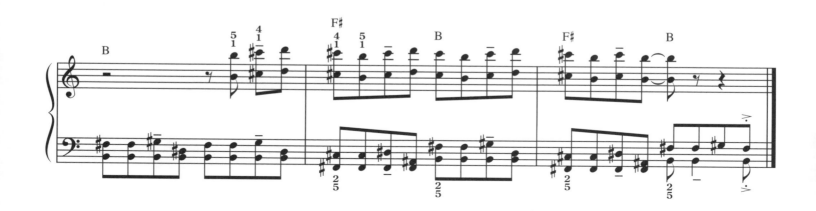

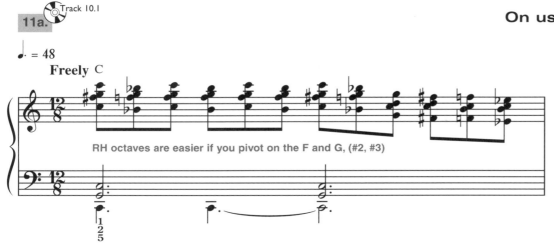

11a. Track 10.1

♩. = 48

Freely C

RH octaves are easier if you pivot on the F and G, (#2, #3)

1 2 5

On using a metronome . . .

"I think it's very important. There was a period in my development where my timing was not good. I tended to rush. I started working with a metronome and now I use it any time I do any kind of scales or exercises. If I'm working on a piece, I'll use it right up to the point where I record it."—C.L.

Sus chords omit the 3rd of the chord

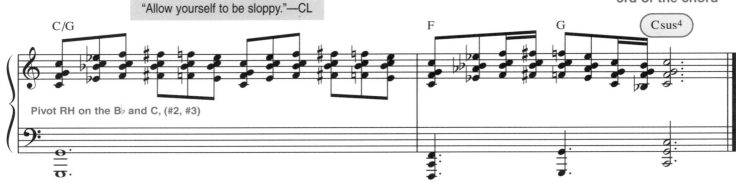

"Allow yourself to be sloppy."—CL

C/G F G Csus⁴

Pivot RH on the B♭ and C, (#2, #3)

11b. Track 10.2

Freely D

RH pivots on the G and A, (#2, #3)

D/A G A Dsus⁴

RH pivots on the C and D, (#2, #3)

On reading music . . .

"If I could go back as a child, I would have learned how to read. To me, the best you can be is if you can both read and improvise."—C.L.

12a. Track 11.1

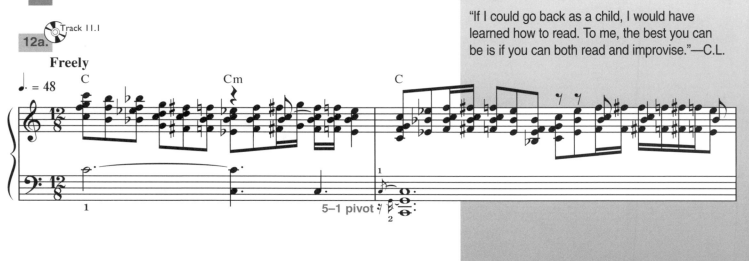

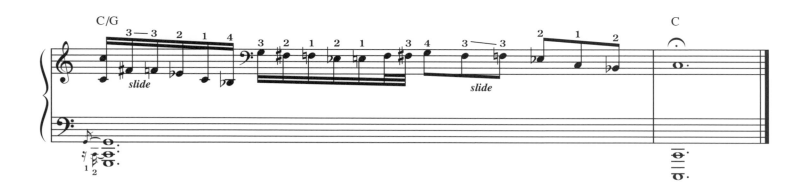

12b. Track 11.2

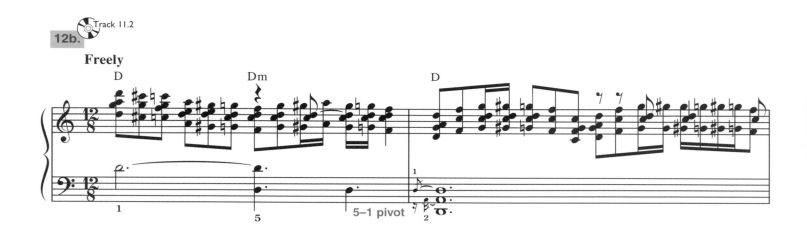

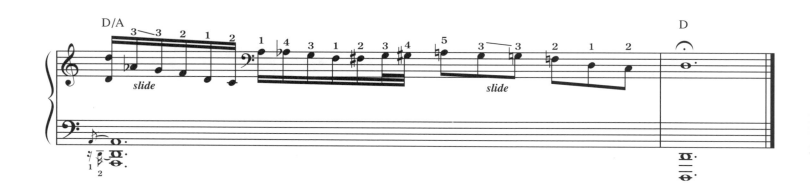

The RH chords below are often called power chords in rock 'n' roll and blues.
The ♭5 (lower the 5th a half step) comes from the blues scale.

Track 12.1

13a.

Track 12.2

13b.

Some of Chuck's style has been influenced by country legend Floyd Cramer.

Chuck recommends listening to Leon Russell,
who often uses gospel type riffs.

"Break up the pattern, change it, don't play
it the same way twice. That makes it more
interesting."—C.L.

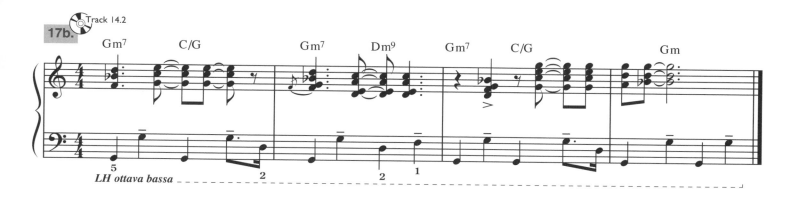

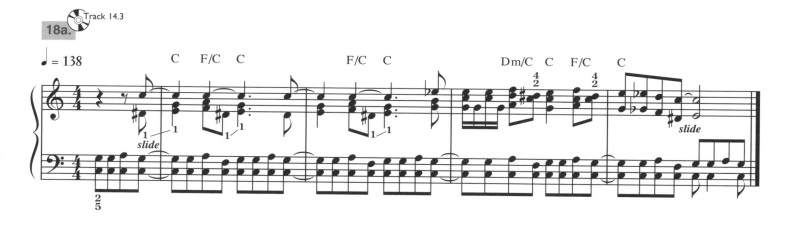

For melodic variety, Chuck adds a scale or chord a 5th above the root.

Track 15.1

19a.

On relative pitch . . .

Track 15.2

19b.

"It's vital if you're jamming with a band and you don't know a particular song or the chord changes. You might be a slight beat behind on the change, but if you have good relative pitch you can make it through."—C.L.

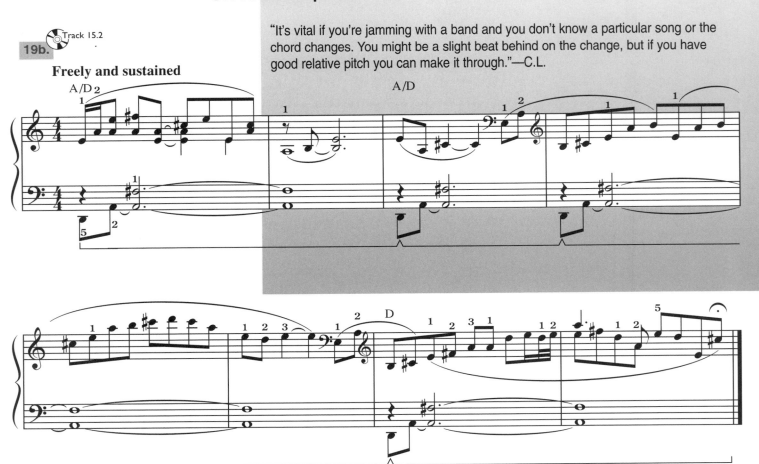

Try playing a scale or chord one whole step above the root
—this will add a nice melodic sound.

20a. Track 16.1

20b. Track 16.2

On mother and creativity . . .

"When I was a kid at the piano, my mother would ask me what a thunder storm would sound like; what would it sound like if the sun came out; if it were raining; if you were scared. It would make me think of musical pictures not just notes and chords."—C.L.

21a. Track 16.3

1-5 pivot on C

21b. Track 16.4

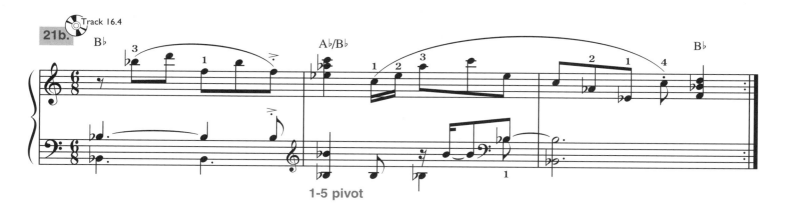

1-5 pivot

PINE TOP BLUES

Track 17

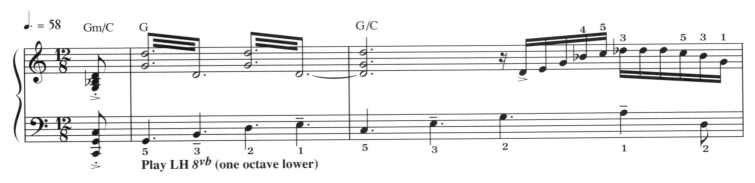

Play LH *8vb* **(one octave lower)**

loco (play LH as written)

8vb - -

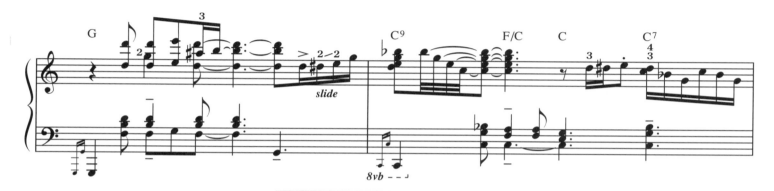

On his skills . . .

"I'm not a classical player. I'm not a jazz player. I'm not a this or a that. What I've done is take a little from all the diverse artists I've had the good fortune to play with. I'm a jack of all trades and a master of none."—C.L.

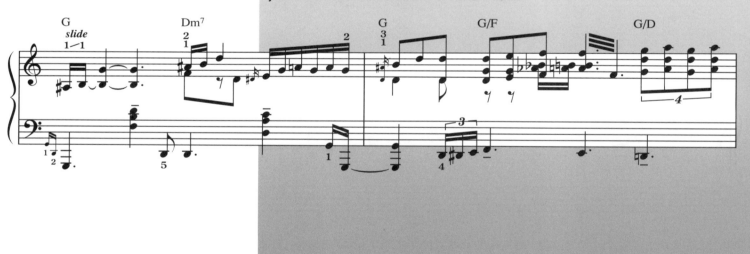

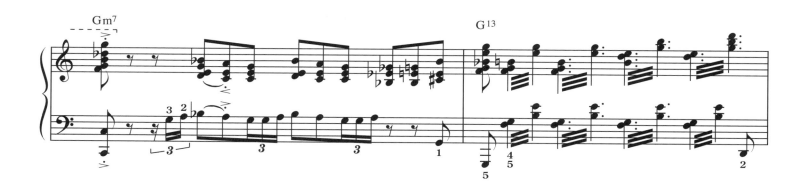

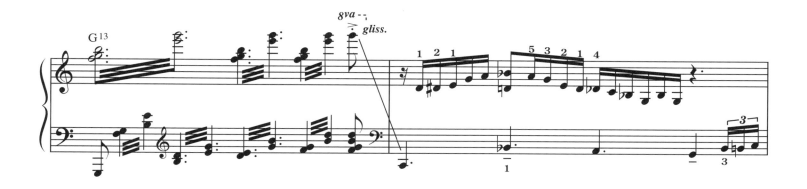

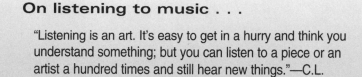

On listening to music . . .

"Listening is an art. It's easy to get in a hurry and think you understand something; but you can listen to a piece or an artist a hundred times and still hear new things."—C.L.

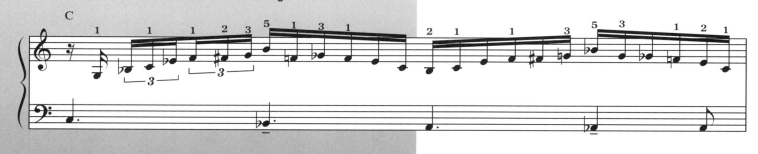

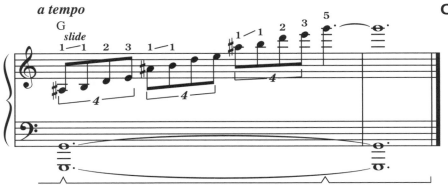

On learning the blues . . .

"Listen to the overall piece, not just the piano licks. Listen to the way the band interacts. Listen to the pain in the vocal and the understanding of the piano along with it. You've got to get a deep feeling and understanding. The music is all about communicating and it's a language that has no boundries."—C.L.

Section 3
Reese Wynans

Even in elementary school, Reese Wynans kept his eyes and ears wide open. Pure survival was one reason: growing up in Sarasota, Florida during the 1950s, Reese was one of seven children and such skills were, no doubt, extremely valuable. But Reese also had a curiosity about music, and he realized it early on. "My father enjoyed playing music after dinner," Reese remembers. "We had an organ and he liked playing *Lawrence Welk- Mitch Miller* easy listening-type ballads. He played beautifully, but I thought that instrument was pretty sleepy back then."

Instead, young Reese's interest was awakened whenever his dad would play

Reese Wynans (right) on stage with Stevie Ray Vaughan
Photo: A. Marc Shamblin/Ambient Life

another instrument. "He would play ragtime on the piano and I liked that," Reese recalls. "I would watch him and think how that was pretty cool. It was fun stuff!"

Reese began taking piano lessons at age six. Despite the fact his parents gave him no choice in the decision, he knew this was something he really wanted to do. "All seven of us kids had to take them. There was simply no question about it," he says emphatically. "You couldn't quit the lessons until it was clear you really weren't going to do something with them—and I was the only one who really loved playing!"

That love continued growing. As Reese got older, he realized he wasn't into sports, so his free time was naturally spent at the keyboard. By junior high, that practice began to pay off. "The fact that I could play ragtime at a school assembly made me a hit, and that seemed pretty cool."

Cool enough to keep him playing, and, as he got a little older, expand his horizons. "When I reached high school, I joined the orchestra and the choir. I also joined

the school stage band. That enabled me to learn more about chords, theory and jazz while I was reading all those nice charts."

The valuable knowledge soon earned Reese his first paying job. He and several of the kids in the stage band put together a smaller version of the ensemble. "We performed in a local hotel. We played nothing but standards. We called ourselves *I Wish You Love.* The band was all guys and we had a girl singer."

While no one would have called the band "cutting edge" in any way, the experience did show Reese that it was possible to play music, have fun, learn something and, at the same time, get paid for it.

And just because the band wasn't playing the hot hits on the rock charts, that didn't mean Reese and the others weren't listening to them. "Yeah, I really wasn't a rocker at all in high school," Reese admits. "But I sure did discover it then. I listened to everybody on the radio. *The Kinks, The Rascals* and *The Rolling Stones*—I thought those were really good bands!"

Reese had also never forgotten a concert he'd attended a few years before. The artist had gotten inside his head and secretly bounced around ever since. "It was *Jerry Lee Lewis,*" Reese remembers fondly, "on the Fourth of July at the Bradenton Auditorium. He was the wildest piano player I'd ever seen and the coolest guy. I was so impressed by his playing and his showmanship. So I bought some of his records and figured out how to play like him."

While rock was making an impression on the teenager, it would still be a few more years until its influences began to surface for others to see. By that time, Reese had graduated from high school and migrated to Tallahassee to attend *Florida State University School of Music.* "I planned on being a music teacher, not a performer," Reese reflects. "That seemed like the best career choice."

He worked hard to perfect his skills. As a music major, Reese now had the opportunity to play virtually around the clock, if that's what he wanted. It was so much better than high school, where he had to squeeze in practice whenever he could. "As a kid, I probably played a half hour a day," Reese estimates. "But in college, I couldn't get enough. I would practice at all hours. I was learning so much playing pieces like the Chopin B-flat Minor Scherzo and the Beethoven sonatas. I was really improving."

Simultaneously, his musical perspective was continuing to broaden. As much as he enjoyed the classics, Reese was increasingly attracted to other sounds. "I had a friend who worked at a local rhythm and blues club," he remembers. "They had a band that didn't have a piano player. I had a Wurlitzer electric piano so they let me sit in with my instrument. This was the 1960s, a great period for soul music. I discovered I loved it and I learned all that stuff."

The learning came easy, thanks to Reese's solid classical training. "I had a good, well-developed ear. I could listen to a song on the radio and determine exactly what chords were being played."

And that talent proved to be an important asset. Reese joined a college rock band called *The Prowlers.* The group gained an on-campus following by playing cover songs at frat parties. "We did whatever was popular at the time. I wasn't a great rock player back then, but, with my ear, I was valuable to the other guys in helping the band work out songs."

Reese listened to everyone and everything he could. He rejected nothing and tried to learn something from whatever he heard. More and more, he became aware of the changing face of rock. "It was progressing from a little band's three-minute song to stretched-out, electric psychedelic music. I thought, 'Wow, this stuff is really great. These people are really expressing themselves.'"

That same need to express oneself soon overcame Reese as well. "After a couple years of college, I decided I just didn't want to teach. So I left school and went out to make a living playing in a rock band."

Actually, several bands, as it turned out. Reese soon was a fixture on the Florida club circuit around Sarasota, Tampa and St. Petersburg. He wasn't getting rich or famous, but he was learning exactly what he wanted to learn. "Most of it was me going around and listening to what my fellow musicians in the area were doing," Reese says. "The most prominent musician around then was *Dickie Betts* over in Jacksonville. *Berry Oakley* was his bass player and their band had a Hammond B-3. I thought that was the coolest sound I had ever heard in my life."

Reese, like so many others, became an instant convert. The "sleepy" instrument of his childhood had awakened with a passion. "I bought "Walk on the Wild Side" by *Jimmy Smith* and started listening to him. He became a major influence immediately. I then went out and bought a small Hammond organ for myself."

Dickie, now a friend, also had Reese's ear. "He was a great guitar player already, particularly with the blues. He did as much to enlighten me about the music as anybody."

So again, Reese started buying records, using that trained ear to learn everything he could. "I still liked rock, but the blues and R&B were getting more and more interesting to me."

B.B. King and *Albert King* were early favorites. But the biggest influences were his new bandmates. "I joined Dickie and Berry's band, *Second Coming.* We had a regular gig at a psychedelic club in Jacksonville called *The Scene.* We did a lot of *Jimi Hendrix* tunes and a lot of blues."

At the time, Reese was still feeling his way along with both the music and the organ. He loved playing the instrument, but in his own mind, he wasn't anywhere close to having developed a style. "Oh, heavens no," Reese laughs. "I had no idea what I was doing. The other guys were playing great and I was just trying to keep up."

Fortunately, Reese had plenty of opportunities to figure it out. The band performed five hours a night, six days a week at The Scene. On Sundays, they did free concerts at a local park. "We just really liked playing," Reese recalls. "Other bands would show up and we'd play for the folks who didn't have enough money to go to the clubs. It was pretty much a gathering of the tribes."

And more than just the local kids took notice. A certain studio musician with a growing reputation of his own started showing up, all the way from Alabama. "His name was Duane Allman," Reese says. "He'd come down from Muscle Shoals. He really liked our music and he would sit in and jam."

As exciting as those Sunday performances were, the big thrill for Reese would come when he and his bandmates went home. "We were all living in the same house in Jacksonville. Duane would stay with us until he had to go back to work at Muscle Shoals. We'd all just play and play."

Those Sunday night sessions were like a magnet. Eventually, Duane began bringing along a drummer he liked from Muscle Shoals. "The guy's name was Jai Johanny Johanson—*Jaimoe*. Then another fellow named *Butch Trucks* started showing up with his band, *The 31st of February*. We had some memorable sessions playing these long, stretched-out jams."

And because Reese was usually the only keyboardist, he played everything with everybody. His confidence and his skills grew markedly during these late night improvs.

But nothing lasts forever. Eventually, another emerging musician showed up who would directly and indirectly affect a number of careers, including Reese's. "Duane's brother, *Gregg Allman*, sang and played the B-3 organ," Reese notes. "The brothers decided to hook up again and hired Dickie, Berry, Butch and Jaimoe. Those guys, of course, became *The Allman Brothers Band.*"

Reese and the rest of Second Coming reorganized and continued as a significant presence in the Jacksonville-Daytona Beach coastal music scene. These were heady and historic days. Second Coming and The Allman Brothers Band commonly shared billing at different area gigs. They were often joined by a third band that was gaining notice. "*The One-Percent*," they called themselves, Reese remembers. "Eventually, they changed their name to *Lynyrd Skynyrd.*"

And far too soon for loyal fans, that remarkable scene became just a memory. The Allmans left for Macon, a recording contract with *Capricorn*, and a star-crossed date with destiny. Likewise, Lynyrd Skynyrd went off on its own fateful path. Second Coming broke up and Reese headed back home to Sarasota. For someone with less perseverance, it could have all ended right there. But Reese already had too much invested to even consider giving up. A phone call to a friend helped refocus the direction of Reese's life forever. "I called Duane in Macon," he recounts. "Duane had been doing sessions with *Boz Scaggs*. Boz was putting together a band and Duane recommended me for the gig."

Reese followed Boz to San Francisco. For the next year, he immersed himself in the city's vibrant music scene. "I got to experience all those great bands—*The Grateful Dead, The Jefferson Airplane, Big Brother and the Holding Company, It's A Beautiful Day* and *Santana*. At that point, I was truly starting to learn how to play."

Reese also developed an interest in the West Coast jazz scene. "I felt like I was maturing," Reese recalls. "I was learning what good jazz was and what good rock was."

And, not coincidentally, people were learning what a talented and diverse musician Reese was. When the gig ended with Boz, Reese returned to Florida. For a while, he supported himself by, once again, playing the club circuit. But he was by now simply too good a player not to have other opportunities come his way. "I got the chance to join a new band *Jerry Jeff Walker* was putting together," Reese says. "So I pulled up roots and moved to Austin."

Those replanted roots took firm hold and Reese's career quickly sprouted. The association with progressive country artist Jerry Jeff benefited all concerned. "We had an excellent band," Reese says. "Jerry Jeff's songs were simple, but he allowed each of us in the band to really, really play."

Four years and five well-received albums later, Reese moved on and joined honky-tonker *Delbert McClinton* and his band. "Finally, I again had the opportunity to get into the blues. With Delbert, we just got on the bus and played."

The road led straight to Reese's best known and most high profile work as a Grammy Award winning member of *Stevie Ray Vaughan's* legendary band, *Double Trouble*. The fame and fortune that followed were earned by the years of hard work and dedication Reese had invested. "I listened to music constantly," he states. "I played music all the time. I learned. I found ideas I liked. I became more fluid."

Stevie Ray's tragic death brought an untimely end to that period of Reese's career—but the habits he established as a young boy still set the course for him now. "These days, I pretty much explore it all," Reese reflects. "I play some blues. I play some sessions. I play in churches. I play in clubs. I'm even playing recitals. The horizon is wide open and I like it that way."

After all this time, Reese Wynans still keeps his eyes and ears wide open.

Licks in the Style of Reese Wynans

Track 18.1

1a.

Review this page to develop the "Reese Wynans style."
A player must have a solid chord, scale and inversion technique to play Reese Wynan's style. His father's
Ragtime playing heavily influenced Reese. You will encounter many "Ragtime slides" in his improv.

Track 18.2

1b.

Track 18.3

1c.

Track 18.4

2a.

"Roll up to chord or its inversion."—RW

Track 18.5

2b.

Reese often warms up playing these scale exercises.

"It's a good way to learn the most important chords in each key."—R.W.

Play the exercise chromatically in all 12 keys.

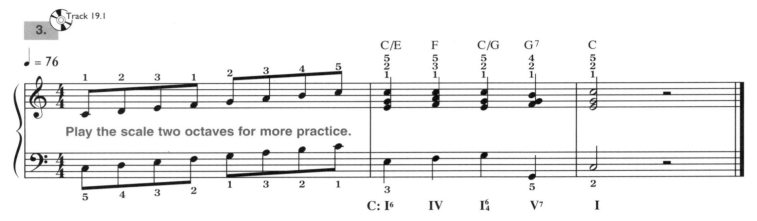

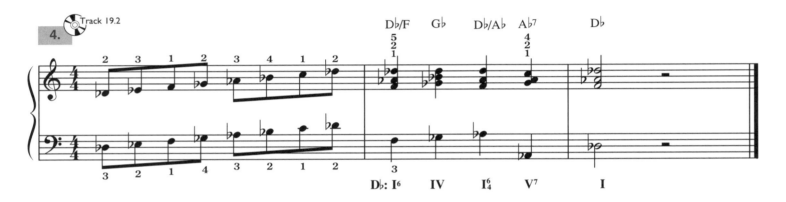

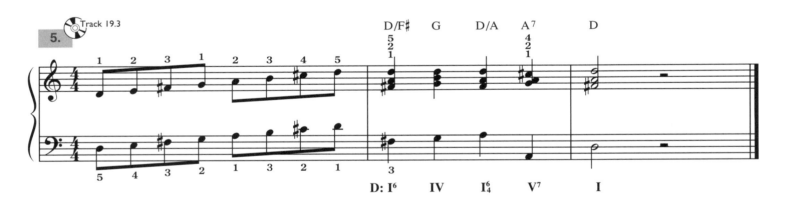

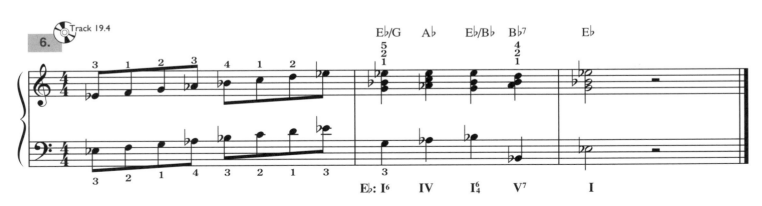

Continue chromatically through B.
See page 15 for fingering.

"I enjoy playing classical music. It's a great way to build and keep up my technique. I use classical in my improv, too."—R.W.

Here's an example of Reese's use of Chopin's *Etude,* Op. 10, No. 10 in his blues improv.

Chopin *Etude*, Op. 10, No. 10

Track 20.1

7a.

Track 20.2

7b.

For a more blues sound, lean on beats 2 and 4.

8a. Track 21.1

On Warming Up . . .

"Scales are a good way to warm up. I love playing the scales through all the keys. I practice scales as fast as I can with no metronome."—R.W.

8b. Track 21.2

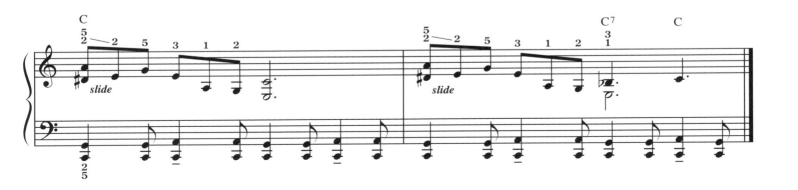

In the style of Reese Wynans playing the big band sound of Count Basie.

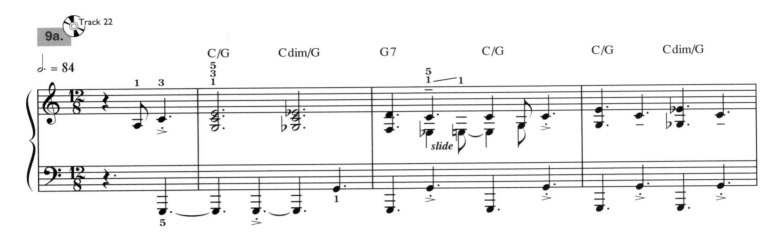

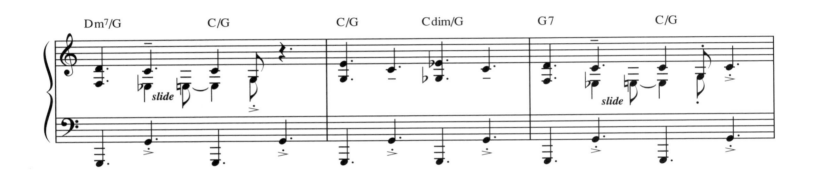

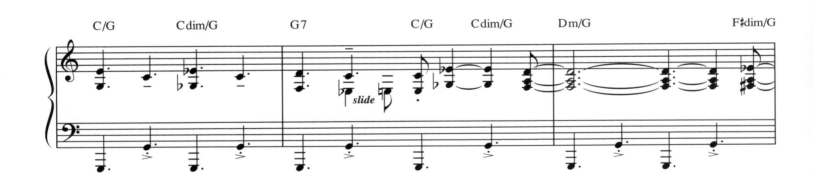

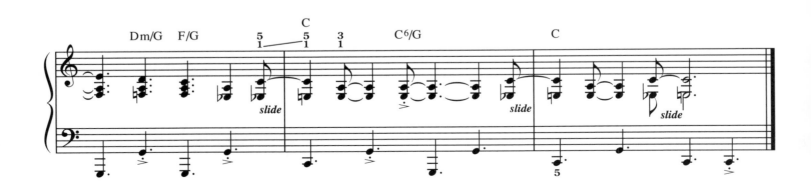

9b. Track 23

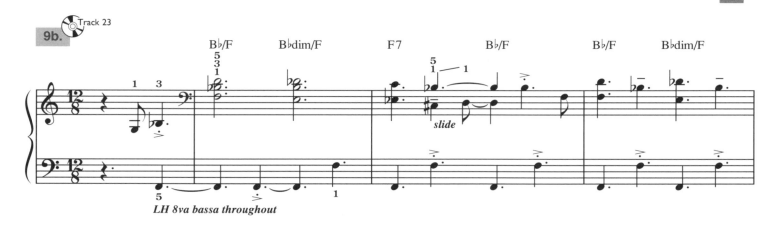

LH 8va bassa throughout

On Developing Skills . . .

"A good ear is invaluable. If you can hear things that are being played on a recording, you can then pick them out and play them."—R.W.

Memphis Blues

In the style of Reese Wynans playing Memphis blues.
Try playing the F blues scale and improvising with the CD.

On Music Theory . . .

"Knowing about theory helps you to be comfortable about where you're at and where you're taking it—but you have to have an idea of where to start and what you want to do with it."—R.W.

MEMPHIS MOOD Track 24

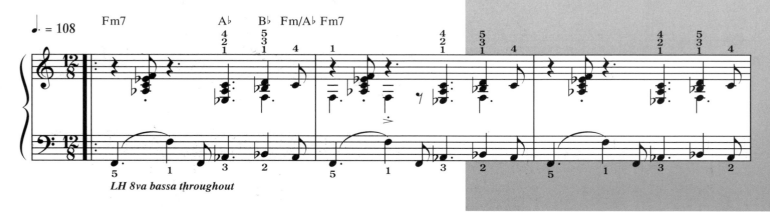

LH 8va bassa throughout

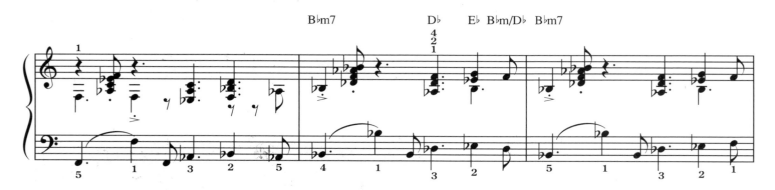

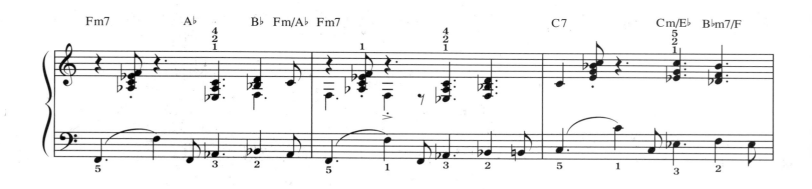

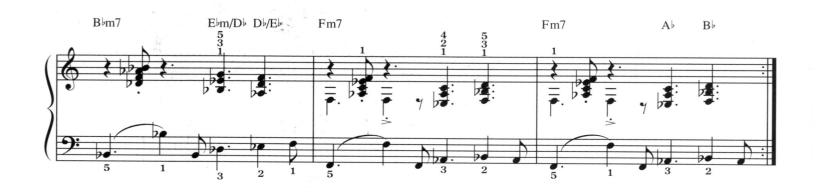

In the style of Reese Wynans playing Memphis blues.

MUD ISLAND BLUES   Track 25

"Memphis blues has a simple LH and strong RH rhythm."—R.W.

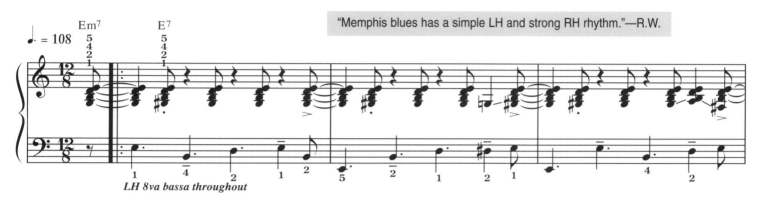

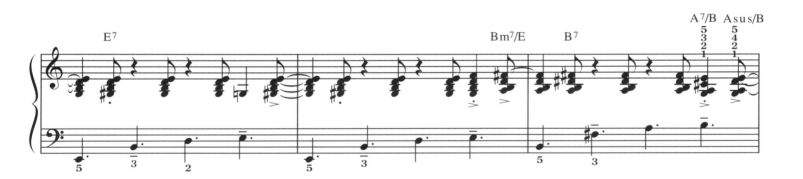

Put the CD on and improvise using the E blues scale, (see page 96).

Delta Blues

In the style of Reese Wynans playing the Delta blues of Louisiana and Mississippi.
Feel in four beats. Lean on beats 2 and 4.

PIANO RED BLUES Track 26

"It's almost like Delta blues doesn't change chords."—RW

 = roll chord

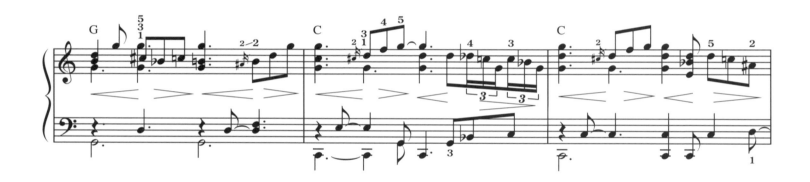

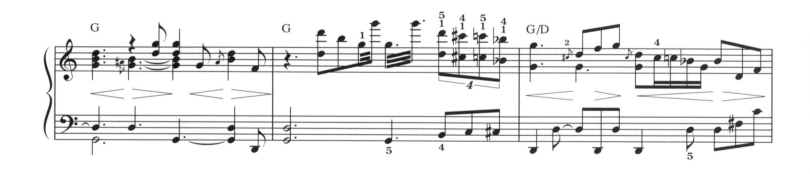

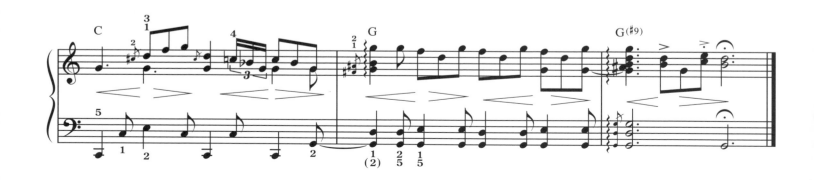

On Borrowing . . .

"It's okay to use other people's ideas in the music business. In playing music, we all borrow ideas from each other. It's perfectly all right to take an idea from someone else if you like it, and then not be afraid to credit them as an influence."—R.W.

Kansas City Blues

In the style of Reese Wynans playing Kansas City blues.

No LH slides: articulate 3 to 3 throughout.

Transpose to G then play a C 12-bar blues.

No LH slides: all hammered and detached.

Transpose to F then play a C 12-bar blues.

12a. Track 28.1

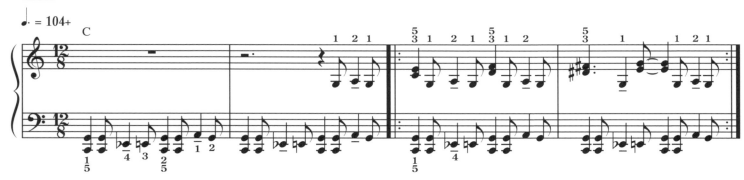

12b. Track 28.2

"When in doubt, play a chromatic scale (half-step movement)."—R.W.

13a. Track 28.3

Feel free to swing it!

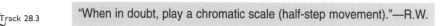
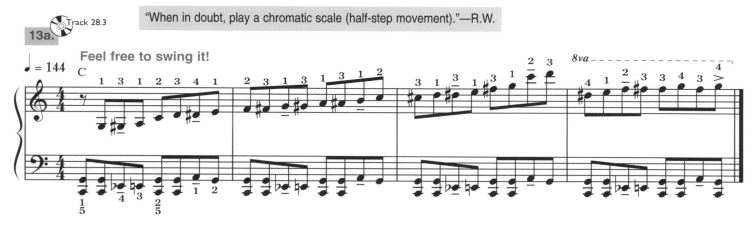

13b. Track 28.4

Chicago Blues

In the style of Reese Wynans playing Chicago style blues.

14a. Track 29.1

"The styles of Otis Spann and Pinetop Perkins' styles are a little more angry sounding."—R.W.

14b. Track 29.2

Barrelhouse

In the style of Reese Wynans playing Barrelhouse blues/rock.

Track 30.1

15a.

On Today's Technology . . .

"If you're starting out today, you have to become very proficient with modern keyboards. You need to learn MIDI and layering effects. If Beethoven were alive today, that's what he'd be doing—he'd be layering his symphonies on the computer."—R.W.

Track 30.2

15b.

How to Develop a Solo: Know Your Theory and Technique

1. First review the key's primary chords and their inversions.

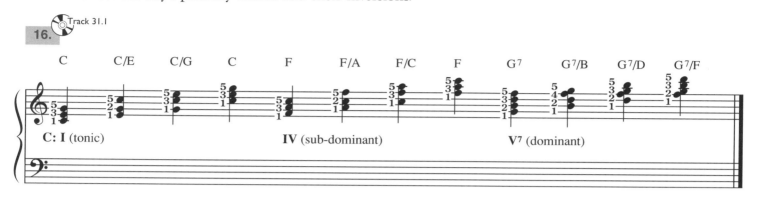

2. Review parallel thirds of all primary chords.

3. Play a simple RH melody using chord tones.
   LH plays intervals of a 4th and 6th.

On Improving . . .

"Listen to music all the time and play all the time. The more you play, the more fluid your ideas will be."—R.W.

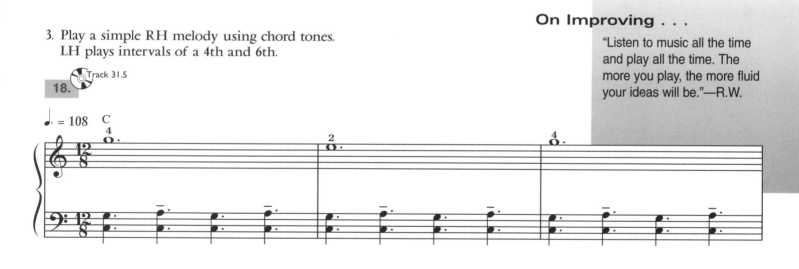

Continue and complete the 12-bar blues form.

4. To further develop a solo, add inversions, 3rds, grace notes and shakes (≩) to the RH.

The LH changes to a shuffle pattern.

19. Track 32.1

"The tremolo/shake gives the improv a Honky-Tonk sound."—R.W.

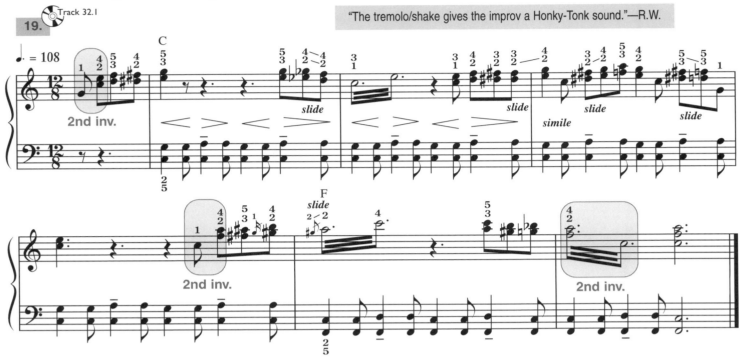

5. Try combining intervals of a 3rd and 6th. Also explore more complex rhythms and polyrhythms.

20. Track 32.2

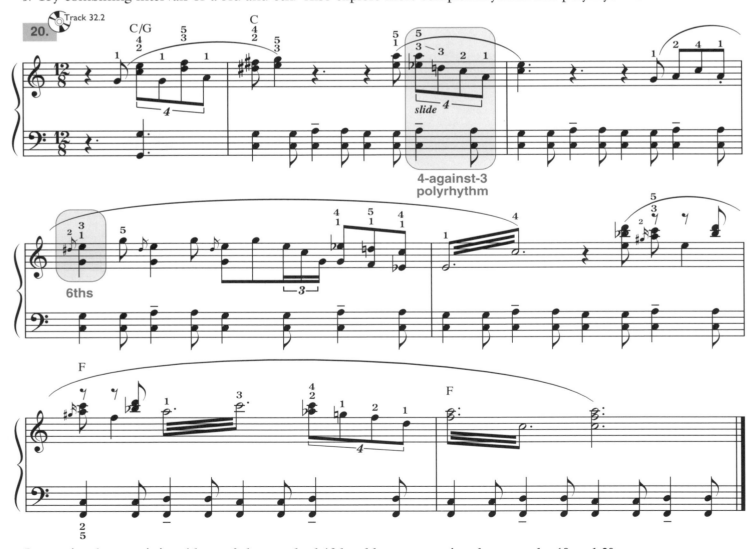

Improvise the remaining 6 bars of the standard 12-bar blues progression for examples 19 and 20.

6. Adding repetition to your solos creates a nice groove.

21. Track 33.1

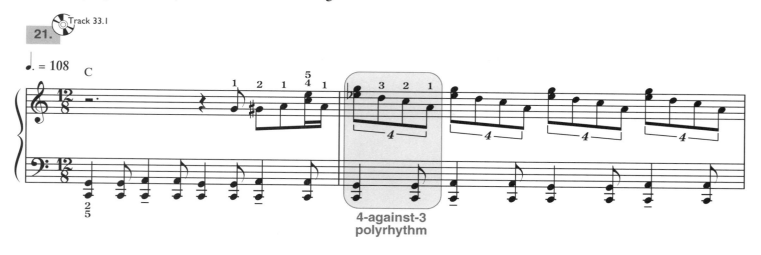

**4-against-3
polyrhythm**

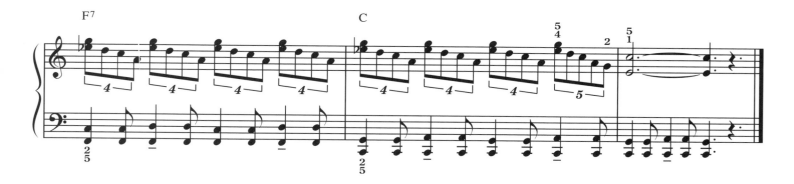

7. Finally, changing octaves or registers will add variety to your improv.

22. Track 33.2

Section 4
Dr. John

Multiple Grammy Award-winning artist Mac Rebennack, a.k.a. Dr. John, comes by it naturally. Born in 1940 and raised smack-dab in the heart of New Orleans' famed Third Ward, young Malcolm, Jr. was surrounded from day one by music and musicians. Virtually his entire immediate family played one instrument or another and served as inspiration for as long as he can remember.

"My maternal grandfather, who sang and hoofed for a while for the *Al G. Fields Minstrel Show* operating out of Mobile, Alabama, was the one who passed the music on to me in a down way for the first time," Mac recalls in his autobiography, *Under a Hoodoo Moon*. "When he was very old, long after he had turned his last act, he used to sit with me on the front porch and sing the charts he had worked in his day."

Those minstrel- and vaudeville-era tunes may have been the beginning of Mac's music education, but others in his family were equally happy to make their contributions in their own particular ways. "One of the first things I remember about my childhood was a white baby grand Kimball piano in the living room," Mac says. "My sister, who was ten years older than I was, used to practice on it and I was hypnotized..."

That instrument apparently held the same attraction for the rest of the family. It was the centerpiece for many evenings of entertainment and education. "My mother, sister, aunties and uncles all gathered around to play," Mac remembers. "They took turns on the piano and sang together."

Mac's Aunt Andre was his special favorite. She seemed to know every song and was more than willing to pass on her knowledge. "She knew how to play 'Texas Boogie' and took the time to teach it to me," he

Photo: Kevin Mazur

recounts. "That was the very first song I learned to play on the piano."

That Mac would remember the event after all these years is remarkable enough...but it's even more amazing put in perspective. It seems Aunt Andre's influence truly rubbed off on him. It's no exaggeration to say that, today, Mac knows literally thousands of tunes, has written countless others, and regularly performs with a list of 120 songs or more at the ready, just in case anybody asks or the spirit moves him. If Mac hears it, he remembers it—and if he can remember it, it's a sure bet he can play it.

Early on, Mac's father helped him cultivate that gift. His dad also liked music, and he happened to own an appliance store. That combination opened the door for Mac to have a unique look inside the rich New Orleans musical scene. "My father used to fix P.A. systems in a lot of the black clubs, and I'd tag along when he did. So I saw early on what was happening. It was at these places that I got my first taste of local acts such as *The Papa Celestin Band, Dave Bartholomew, The Basin Street Six, Professor Longhair*, and a hundred others."

Mac's father also stocked his store with the records of those musicians he liked and saw. When Mac was there, he made sure something was playing on the phonograph; and, over time, he was exposed to much of the best in musical forms as varied as gospel, bebop, jazz, hillbilly, pop, R&B and blues.

Taking a cue from his father, Mac also started a record collection of his own at home. Likewise, he soon developed an eclectic taste that ranged from *Roy Rogers* to *Louie Armstrong* and everybody in between. "Pianists like *Albert Ammons* and *Pete Johnson* made me want to play," Mac remarks. "Their fast boogie—'Roll 'Em Pete' and 'Swanee River Boogie'—excited me and I thought, 'I want to be like that; that's what I want to do.'"

Still, all the exposure had its down side, too. The abundance of great piano players in New Orleans could be intimidating, especially to a young boy just starting out. "How was I ever going to compete with killer players like *Tuts Washington? Salvador Doucette? Herbert Santina?*" Mac reasoned. "So I began to pick up on the guitar players."

Over the next few years, Mac would broaden his musical base with private guitar lessons from *Roy Montrell* and *Walter "Papoose" Nelson*, strong and soulful players who had both worked with *Fats Domino.* "To point me in the right direction, Papoose insisted I learn to read music, and got me to listening to other guys, like *Billy Butler* and *Mickey Baker*," Mac points out. "These two were defining the sound of rhythm and blues guitar at the time."

And such good teachers were everywhere in the Crescent City of the 1950s. The R&B club scene down on Canal Street offered opportunities galore for someone with talent, no matter what age. "I loved hanging around with those guys, and I learned a lot from them," Mac says. "They played every standard in the world; they had moves for songs that transported them into another dimension."

Mac also took to hanging around the local recording studios. It was at the famed *Cosimo Matassa's J&M Studios* where he first befriended his piano idols *Huey "Piano" Smith, James Booker, Allen Toussaint* and, of course, the one-and-only Professor Longhair.

Such exposure helped separate Mac from the crowd. By his early teens, he was gaining a reputation around the city for both his playing and songwriting. Labels such as *Speciality Records* liked his tunes and passed them on to artists, including *Little Richard* and *Art Neville*. "I hustled over...and gave them what I'd been working on at school. I scored with them on a bunch of these songs," Mac recounts. "I didn't make much...maybe 30 or 40 dollars each. But that was decent pocket money for a high school kid, and having my songs recorded and published was pretty heavy stuff."

Heavy enough to create a major shift in Mac's thinking. Although he was enrolled in New Orleans' prestigious Jesuit High School, his mind was elsewhere. Playing the school dance circuit with his band, *The Spades*, just wasn't enough. The lure of the street and the business of being a professional musician simply held too strong an attraction. During his junior year, he left school for good.

The next few years were filled with ups and downs. Questionable decisions marred aspects of Mac's personal life, but he never once wavered from his desire to be the best musician he could be. Through it all, he kept listening, learning, and playing, playing, playing.

A grueling combination of road gigs, songwriting and session work paid the bills. "We might cut a session in the morning, do a gig in the French Quarter that afternoon, cut another session that night after the gig, play a late-night gig after the session, then get up the next day to make a gig somewhere up in Mississippi or Arkansas," Mac remembers. "Our schedules would be crazy."

In the late 1950s, Mac branched out as an artists and repertory rep for *Johnny Vincent's Ace Records,* where he produced sessions for New Orleans musicians including *Earl King, Sugarboy Crawford* and *Alvin "Red" Tyler.* That was followed by stints as a songwriter, session player and producer for a number of labels, including *Minit, Ric and Ron A.F.O.,* and *ABC Records.* "It was a strange and wonderful time to work in New Orleans as a musician," Mac recalls fondly.

But, to borrow a line from Bob Dylan, the times, they were a-changin'. With the coming of a new decade, the musical scene in New Orleans—-and the business nationally—-changed dramatically. By 1965, Mac and many of his old partners had moved to Los Angeles to make a new start.

He found session and songwriting work in abundance. Over the next few years, Mac worked with such well-known names as *Phil Spector, Bobby Darin, The O-Jays, The Monkees* and *Sonny & Cher.* He also spent more time than he would have preferred with a succession of one-hit wonders, but the bad times helped him appreciate the good all the more. "That's why it was a real treat for me to do the occasional *Motown* session in L.A. or to record with *Johnny "Guitar" Watson, Larry Williams,* or even Little Richard, " Mac says. "With that kind of cat, sessions had that old New Orleans feel."

And it was the desire to maintain that feel which ultimately led to Mac's big breakthrough. He and his small group of "New Orleans exiles," as they called themselves, longed to do an album showcasing the music they knew and loved. When the chance came to grab free studio time during some Sonny & Cher sessions, they went for it. Mac knew exactly what he wanted to do. "I had always thought we could work up an interesting New Orleans-based concept behind the persona of the legendary con-jureman *Dr. John*," Mac explains. "This would not only allow for a dash of gris-gris (home-brew magic charms) in the lyrics and a view of an untapped side of New Orleans, but would also let us musicians get into a stretched-out New Orleans groove."

Even a visionary like *Ahmet Ertegun* of *Atlantic Records* wasn't exactly sure what kind of gumbo the good doctor had cooked up, but he knew the flavor was unique. He was willing to gamble that somewhere out there was an audience hungering for a taste of "the fonk," as Dr. John would say.

This first album, appropriately titled *Gris-Gris*, was both a critical and commercial success in 1968. To meet the public demand for more, Mac had to pull together a stage act in short order. And while things were sudden-ly happening very quickly, Mac was still well aware of exactly what he wanted to do. "We weren't in it just to play," he reveals. "We wanted to put on a show. And we were going to show these people New Orleans style."

At long last, Mac—or Dr. John the Night Tripper—was able to let the world in on what he and his band-mates had been seeing and hearing and experiencing their entire lives. "What I wanted was entertainment for the eyes as well as the ears," Mac states. "It was a kick to bring back that idea of showmanship to the rock and roll era, where at the time there was little old-style show biz happening."

Dr. John would go on to do five more albums for Atlantic, each one digging deeper into the rich mother lode of New Orleans music. A wider and wider audience was exposed to the full range of R&B, rock, blues, jazz, funk, dixieland, gospel and boogie-woogie that flavors Dr. John's tasty gumbo.

His biggest commercial success came in 1973 with the release of *In The Right Place*. Produced by long-time friend Allen Toussaint, the album

Dr. John and Karen Ann Krieger

featured the hit singles "Right Place, Wrong Time" and "Such A Night."

In the years following, Dr. John's reputation and talents continued to grow. Numerous recordings and tours, megastar sessions with the likes of *Eric Clapton*, *John Lennon*, and *The Rolling Stones*, plus numerous commercial jingles kept his legions of fans entertained and wanting more.

Following a difficult period of personal problems that peaked in the 1980s, Dr. John emerged from the fog in 1989 to record the album *In A Sentimental Mood*. This collection of blues and saloon standards won Mac his first Grammy for his duet with singer Rickie Lee Jones on "Makin' Whoopie." Three years later, he earned his second such award for *Goin' Back To New Orleans*, an album featuring an all-star line-up of home-town heroes, including *Danny Barker, Al Hirt, Pete Fountain, Chuck Carbo, The Neville Brothers* and long-time friend Red Tyler.

But as nice as they look on the mantel, awards and the trappings of success aren't what it's all about for Mac Rebennack. It always has been, and always will be, about the music. To this day, it's really no different for Mac than it was when he sat on his parents' front porch as a young boy and listened to his grandfather teach him his first song. "Music is something no one person owns," Mac muses. "Like a field holler or a second-line rhythm, it hovers in the air for a lingering beat and passes away, living through us only for a moment. We can give it our spin, but then we have to let go and pass it on."

So on he goes, keeping that music he loves alive and sharing his knowledge with anyone interested enough to listen.

Somewhere—-on a heavenly front porch, perhaps—-Mac's grandfather is smiling.

Photo: Bonnie Smith

Dr. John: the New Orleans Style

Play through these ideas to get a feel for Dr. John's style.

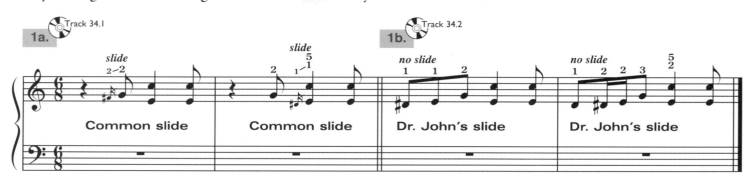

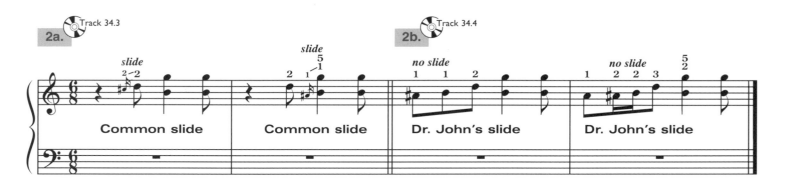

Dr. John's New Orleans style includes many licks with groupings of three or four notes.

Licks in the Style of Dr. John

Track 35

FAMILY TIME BLUES

No LH slides throughout

*Dr. John plays both E♭ and E♮ with finger #3. This ensures a detached sound.

"Turnarounds are a big part of the New Orleans style.
I listened to a lot of piano and guitar players to develop
my style.—Dr. J.

5a.

5b.

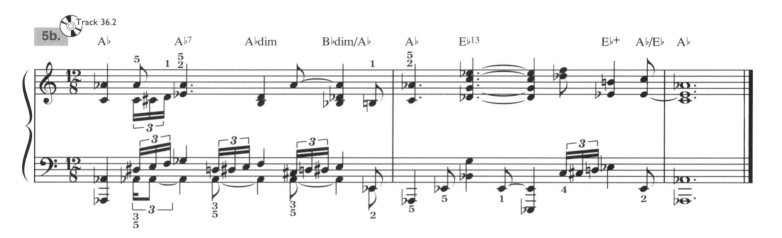

6a.

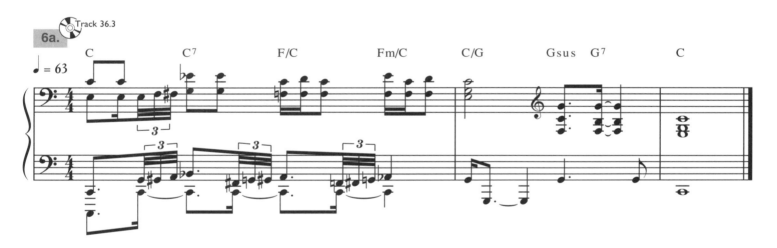

6b.

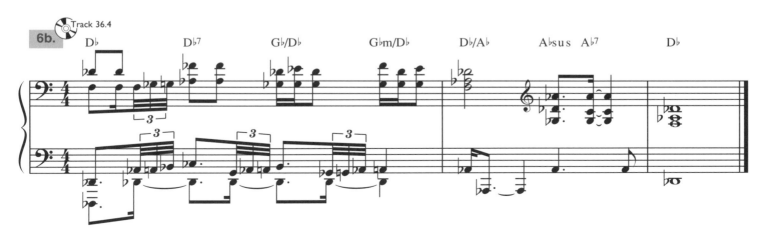

7a. Track 37.1

Freely and slow

7b. Track 37.2

Freely and slow

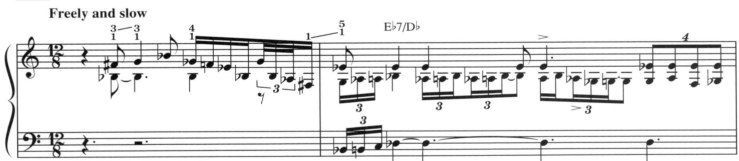

On Songwriting . . .

8a. Track 38.1

> "You can get the idea for blues by playing a blues piece where there's a million different versions by different piano players."—Dr. J.

8b. Track 38.2

Dr. John's style includes many left-hand 10ths.

9a. Track 38.3

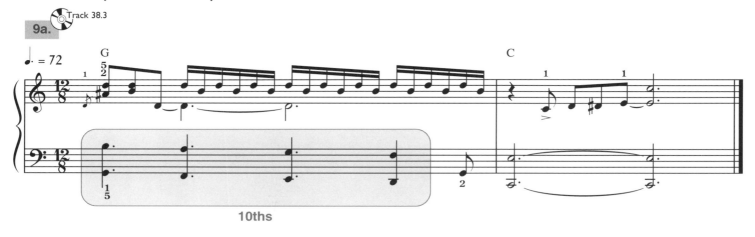

10ths

9b. Track 38.4

10a. Track 39.1

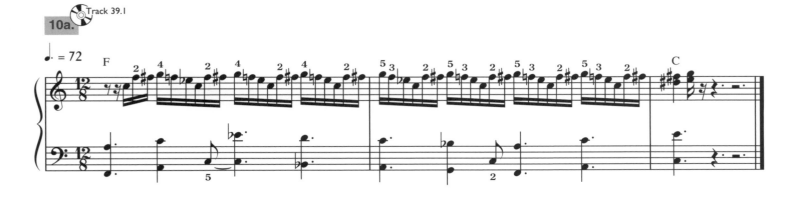

10b. Track 39.2

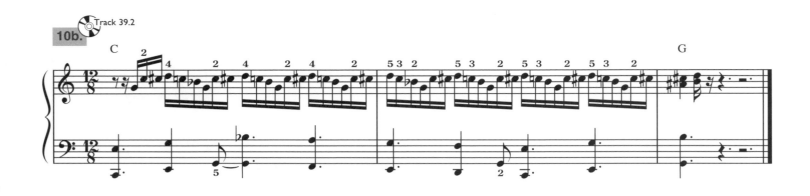

11a. Track 39.3

11b. Track 39.4

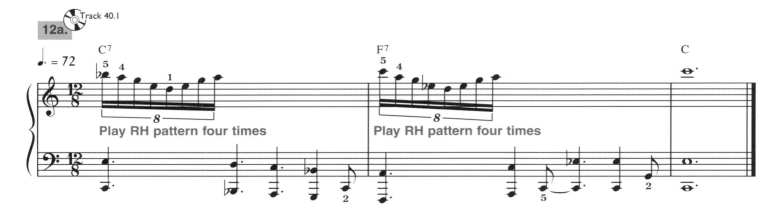

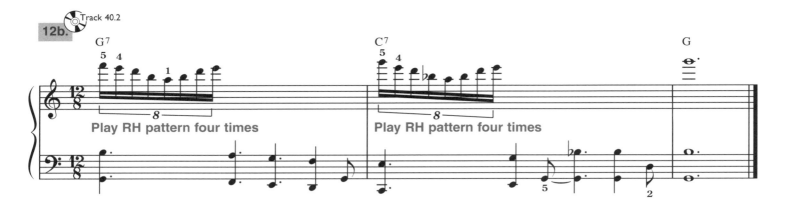

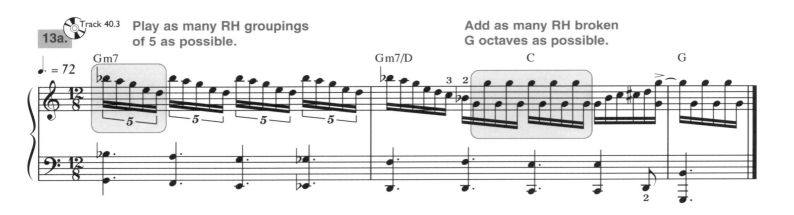

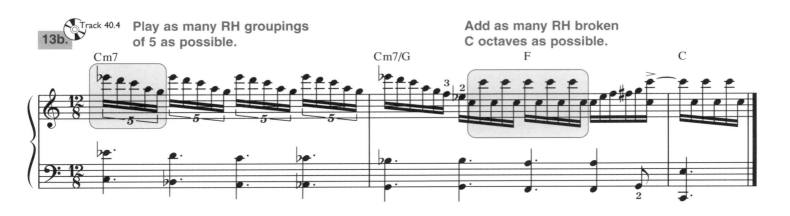

Track 41.1

14a.

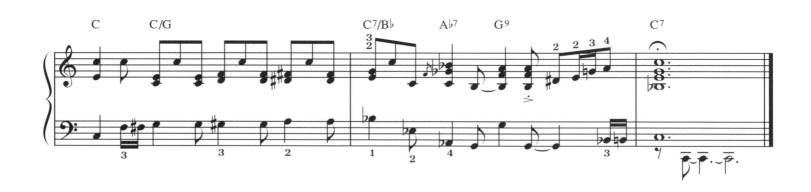

Track 41.2

14b.

On Studying Music . . .

"Kids should study whatever they can. They should just find out what they're interested in and keep going. They should be open-minded and run with it. That's what music is all about."—Dr. J.

Dr. John playing in the style of Rhythm and Blues. Dr. John uses many tritone substitutions: A♭7 can substitute for D7 because their 3rds and 7ths are the same (A♭ **C** E♭ **G♭** and D **F♯** A **C**).

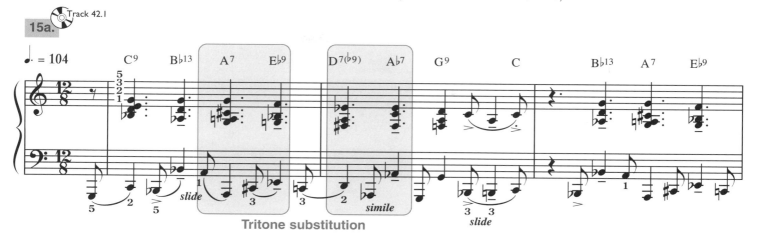

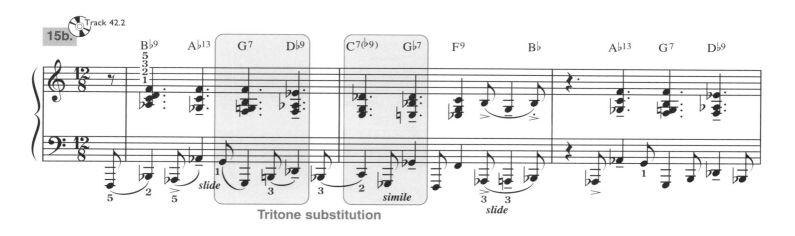

These are Dr. John's favorite licks learned while watching others perform.

16a.

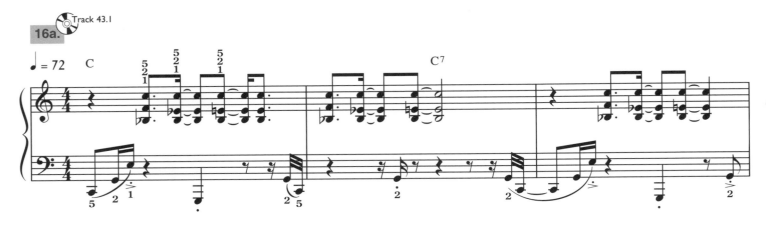

16b.

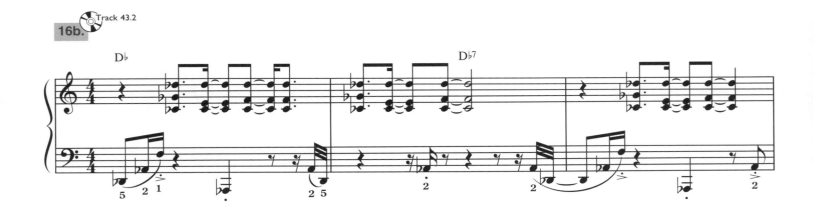

In the style of Dr. John playing Huey "Piano" Smith.

17a. Track 44.1

17b. Track 44.2

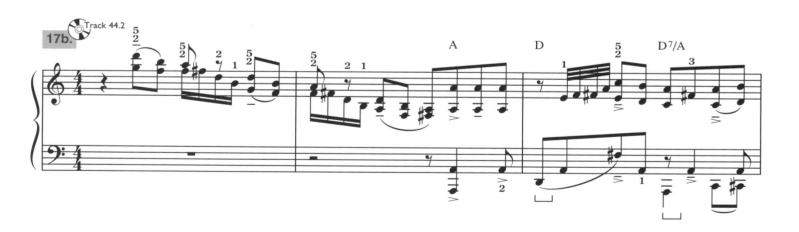

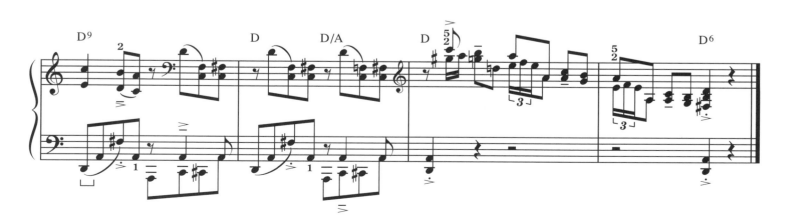

The Basic 8-Bar Blues Progression

Dr. John playing in the New Orleans style of Professor Longhair.
8-bar blues: **I I IV IV I V I I**
Lean on beats 2 and 4 for a more bluesey sound.

THE PROFESSOR'S BLUES Track 45

On Learning to Play . . .

"Get your ears unplugged. Get your mind unplugged. Listen to everything and develop your ability to do what you're here for."—Dr. J.

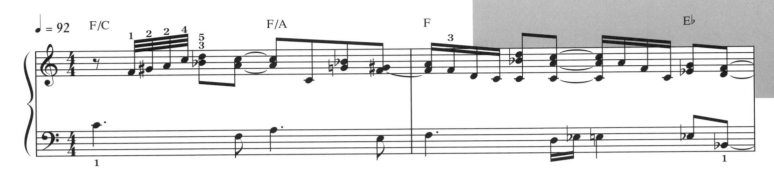
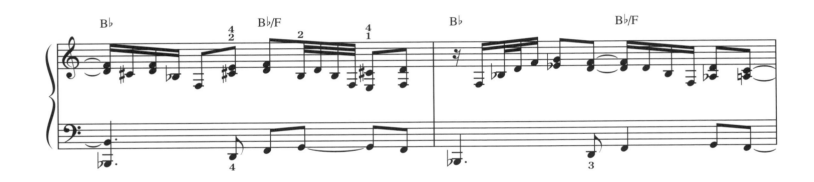

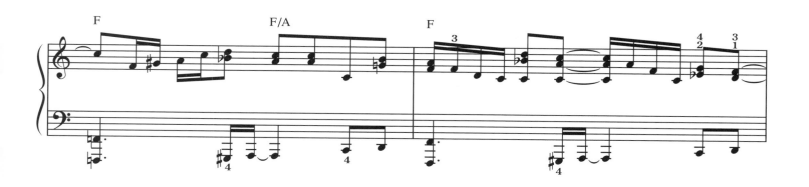

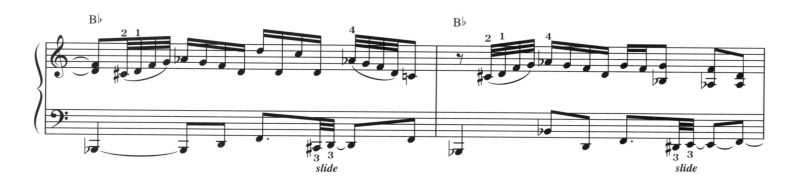

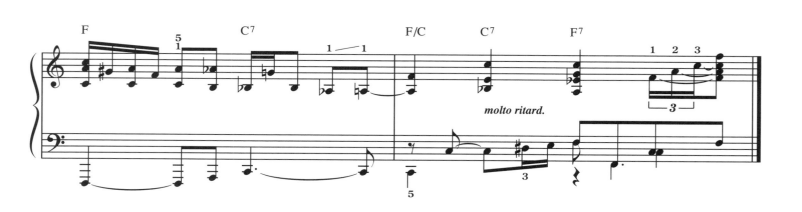

Dr. John playing in the style of Fats Domino.

FAT CITY BLUES   Track 46

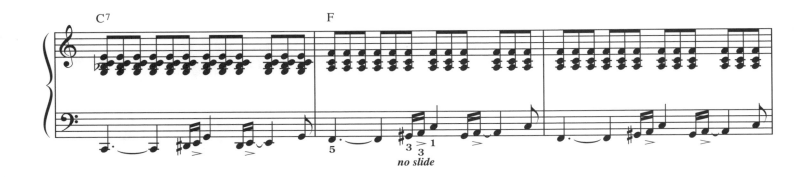

Try holding the RH F through the entire measure.

Try holding the RH E♭ through the entire measure.

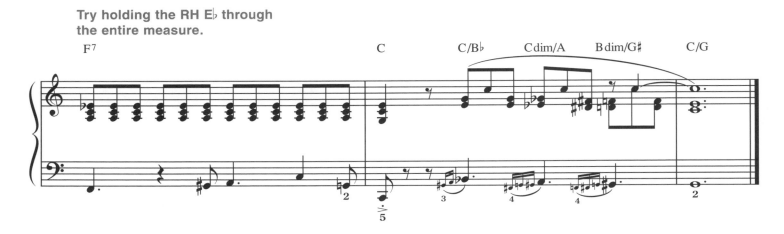

Section 5
The Hammond B-3 Organ

A 1963 split-window Vette...a pair of faded jeans...a Hammond B-3 organ...

True classics are always in style.

Sixty years after *Laurens Hammond* created his first B-3 at his Chicago factory, this coveted instrument is still used at recording studios and live gigs everywhere.

"I'm so comfortable with it," raves rock and blues legend *Al Kooper.* "It's a great instrument that never went away."

The B-3 is big, heavy (400 pounds), and technology has passed it by—but there's nothing quite like the tonal quality this powerhouse generates. Hooked to a massive tube-amplifier equipped *Leslie 122 Speaker*, this monster combo can nail you to the wall. It rightfully remains a favorite of world-class players who know the sound they want and how to get it.

"I love it," Kooper adds. "I've made it my life's work and I've always wished that people could know what's involved in the instrument and the thought process behind it."

So what is the secret?

To begin with, the B-3 has two 61-note keyboards (or manuals). There are a variety of built-in special effects including "percussion" and several different "chorus" and "vibrato" effects. Each manual has two sets of nine stops (or drawbars). Each drawbar slides in or out from 0 to 8, adding specific harmonics. When you literally "pull out the stops" (yes, that's the origin of the expression), you'll hear the largest possible sound.

The big Leslie external tone cabinet has a lot to do with that powerful sound. Approximately six feet tall, the Leslie contains two rotating treble horns at the top, a bass woofer inside, and two more rotating horns

down below. The horns rotate continuously, either slow or fast. When the fast switch is activated on the B-3, the horns speed up and create that huge Hammond vibrato musicians and listeners love.

These days, many manufacturers, including Hammond, market a variety of digitally based portable organs and keyboards that emulate the sound of the original B-3. A variety of these new instruments incorporate full MIDI. But despite the choices that are available today, the classic B-3 remains popular and stands alone in the hearts of musicians everywhere.

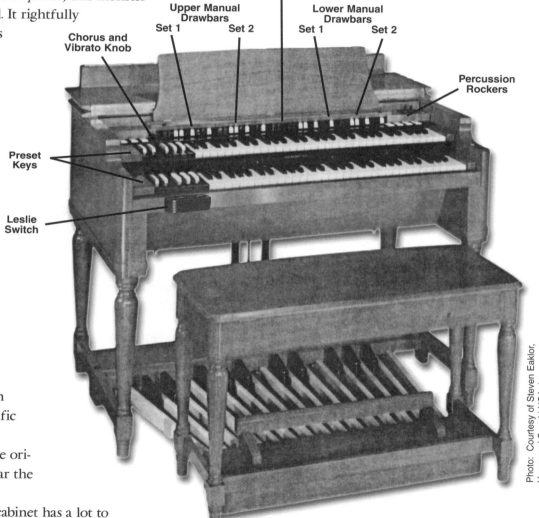

2 Pedal Drawbars
Upper Manual Drawbars — Set 1 / Set 2
Lower Manual Drawbars — Set 1 / Set 2
Chorus and Vibrato Knob
Percussion Rockers
Preset Keys
Leslie Switch

Photo: Courtesy of Steven Eaklor, Hammond Suzuki USA, Inc.

Section 6
Al Kooper

If you saw the movie *Forrest Gump*, you know already that the title character was a unique fellow with special gifts and an uncanny knack for showing up everywhere at just the right time. If something big was happening, Forrest was somewhere in the scene. Sometimes, he *was* the scene.

Of course, that was just a movie, and people like the aforementioned Mr. Gump don't really exist, right? Well, in the world of American rock and contemporary blues, there is one individual who seems to have "been there and done that" with just about everybody—and even today, after some 40 years in the biz, the guy keeps popping up and surprising people at every turn.

Keyboardist and guitarist Al Kooper is the type of person you want to sit down with and just listen to him talk. In fact, that's a big part of the appeal these days to his college students at the prestigious *Berklee School of Music* in Boston. What those students want to learn is what Al's been doing since the early days of rock 'n' roll. As a performer, a producer, and a discoverer of new talent, Al has left his mark on popular music and helped lead it to where it is today.

Here are just a few of the names he's been associated with over the years...

As a player: *Blood, Sweat & Tears, The Blues Project, Jimi Hendrix, Bob Dylan, The Rolling Stones, The Who, George Harrison, Tom Petty, Trisha Yearwood.*

As a producer: *Ray Charles, B.B. King, Lynyrd Skynyrd, Rick Nelson, Stephen Stills, Mike Bloomfield, The Tubes.*

As a songwriter: *The Beastie Boys, Ten Years After, Gene Pitney.*

Keeping this list short is tough. A complete listing would literally take pages—and it continues to grow, possibly even as you read this. It seems music will always have Al Kooper, just as Al has always had music.

In 1950, Al was just six years old and living in Queens, New York with his parents when he discovered the piano. "They took me to a friend's home that had one," he remembers. "I had never had access to one before and I sat down fascinated by it. In an hour, I was playing the number one song at the time, 'The Tennessee Waltz.'"

Al's parents were understandably impressed, but they were also financially unable to afford a piano so that their gifted child could properly develop his skills. Taking a cue from their son, they, too, began thinking creatively. "So we would visit other friends who had pianos," Al reminiscences. "I would tag along and sit and play for the entire length of their visit. I would play the hits of the day instinctively by ear."

Photo: Jim Herrington

A few years and numerous visits later, Al's folks happily purchased a spinet for their son. Lessons followed, but with mixed results and a succession of teachers. "Finally, they got me a teacher by the name of *Ann Sernas*," Al warmly recollects. "She got me started, if anyone did. She actually asked me what I wanted to play. She would then get the sheet music and we would study that. I wanted to learn the hits, songs like 'Love is a Many-Splendored Thing' and 'Three Coins in a Fountain.' It was such a breakthrough!"

Al's continuing interest in the hot hits soon moved him in another direction—one that wasn't particularly pleasing to his parents. The sound of popular music was changing. "At the age of 12, I fell under the spell of *Elvis*," says Al, "and I turned my back on the keyboard in favor of the guitar. I got a cheap Sears single pick-up electric and I taught myself. I'd play along to Elvis, *Chuck Berry* and *Rick Nelson* records for hours every day."

Al didn't know it then, but that beloved black and silver ax would soon become the key that unlocked the door to the rest of his long musical life.

But first came hours and hours of practice over the next year. Al and three friends even started a band they called *The Aristo-Cats*. Al played both guitar and piano. Gigs playing cover tunes at the local temples and churches netted the guys a cool ten bucks apiece. Gas was cheap since their parents drove them there and back. However mortifying that might have been, Al was still living large for a seventh-grader, and it was all because of his emerging talents on the two instruments.

Brimming with confidence—and more than a little naivete—Al then took a bold step that would have positively paralyzed many musicians of more years and experience. Shortly before entering the eighth grade at the ripe old age of 13, Al followed a buddy he had met at summer camp into New York City. The pair headed straight for the uncontested heart of the American music industry, located on a five-block stretch of Broadway. Their destination: the now-legendary *1650 Building*. A sign outside read "The best known address in the entertainment field." Al remembers it well. "An exaggeration, perhaps, but ironically not by all that much. I wish it just said, 'The place where rock 'n' roll exploded.'"

And with it, young Al Kooper's career. Al's summer camp bud, *Danny Schactman*, was a guitar player a couple years his senior. Dan, the grizzled veteran, actually had a record out and had acquired a manager, *Leo Rogers*, whose office was in the 1650 Building. On that thin thread, Al was able to walk in the door past the usual crowd of hopefuls hanging around and audition as a guitarist for a skeptical Leo. "I wailed out reasonable facsimiles of Link Wray's 'Rumble' and 'Rawhide' on my Sears electric," Al recalls. "To my surprise, it made everyone smile. I was offered a job that very night, backing a group called *The Casuals*."

That performance in a Long Island high school gym netted the eager young musician a heretofore unimagined 15 dollars or so. A life's work had begun. "It seemed like heaven," Al states. "From then on, whenever I had money in my pocket, I'd become the phantom of 1650 Broadway. If I was lucky enough to be hanging around at the right time, I might even get a shot at earning my subway fare back home for the week."

And soon, being in the right place at the right time began leading to more high-profile gigs. A group named *The Royal Teens* needed a new guitar player. The band had already scored big with a national hit called "Short Shorts," so the job was highly coveted. When the call came into Leo's office, 14-year-old Al was standing right there, and The Royal Teens soon had themselves a new member.

The conflicts inherent in late nights, rock 'n' roll and schoolwork all raised concerns with Al's parents. A disagreement with Leo Rogers led to their disapproval of the whole rock scene. Wise or not, Al became adept at inventing excuses and covers so that he could continue gigging with the Royal Teens.

Soon, that began to wear thin as the band cooled off and the money dried up. Al, now 16 and looking for new challenges, took a short walk down Broadway to the upstairs music offices in the *1697 Building* (which was also the ground floor home of *The Ed Sullivan Show* and later became the TV home of the *Late Show with David Letterman*).

It was in the funky atmosphere of 1697 Broadway where Al hooked up with a new manager, *Jim Gribble*. "Jim manipulated the fortunes of some of the legendary local doo-wop heroes, among them, *The Passions* and *The Mystics*," Al observes. "He was incredibly patient and seemed to take genuine interest in his musicians...I was writing songs and hustling into whatever sessions I could, and Jim's office provided a much more receptive atmosphere."

And a competitive one, to boot. Everyday, Jim's outer office was packed with players looking for a chance. Al showed up regularly after school, and he quickly grew wise beyond his years. "The point of the game was to make yourself as conspicuously available as possible," he reveals. "What we were all grasping at was the opportunity for involvement. My philosophy was that you couldn't afford the luxury of trying to be in the right place at the right time. You had to be every place at every time and hope that you might wind up anyplace at all."

When Jim unfortunately passed away, Al was on the move again, right back to the 1650 Building. He sold some songs to a publisher, *Aaron Schroeder*, and happened to be in the office when a young, unknown talent named *Gene Pitney* walked in the door. With the help of Schroeder, Pitney would later achieve major stardom with songs like "Town Without Pity" and "The Man Who Shot Liberty Valance," but that day, he was just another kid looking for a break——at least until he cranked it up. "The guy sat down at the piano and proceeded to mesmerize us for two uninterrupted hours with his incredible songs and bizarre voice," Al recalls. "He was an original, and the impact on me was like hearing soul music for the first time."

As Gene Pitney's star rose, Al cultivated a strong friendship. He would grow as a result. "Unconsciously, I assimilated aspects of Gene's style," Al reflects. "I started to sing like him. I started to play the piano like him. I started to write songs that only he could have inspired. At that time, I was still a lump of clay in search of a benevolent pair of hands, and his proved to be as strong and artistic as were needed."

So while the education of "Real World Al" was progressing quite swimmingly, "Collegiate Al" was having his problems. By this time, he was enrolled at the nearby *University of Bridgeport* and he was finding it a difficult fit. "I had the feel, but not the fingers required of a piano major," Al reasons. "And the concept of a guitar major had not yet occurred to the faculty, so this rock 'n' roll animal wound up majoring in bass fiddle.

And fiddle, he did. At the end of the school year, Al called it quits.

In reality, he had been spending most of his time back in the city working toward his dream. He wrote ghost arrangements, tried his hand at producing song demos, and teamed up with lyricists *Bob Brass* and *Irwin Levine* to write songs. That matching had been the idea of publisher *Hal Webman*, who owned *We Three Music*. Brass and Levine had already penned a couple of hits for *The Shirelles* and *The Jarmels*, but

they needed to collaborate with a quality musician. Hal Webman thought Al was the man, but the man himself wasn't quite sure. "However, I was always one for challenges," Al admits, "and I took on the task of catching up to their level of professionalism."

The collaboration was a comfortable one for all three. A few of their songs were recorded during their days with We Three Music, but it was after the trio decided to free-lance their material that success arrived——and in a way that surprised them.

Brass-Kooper-Levine had written a rhythm & blues song with *The Drifters* in mind. That didn't happen. Instead, the tune was purchased by old friend Aaron Schroeder, who would soon hire the trio as staff writers for his company. Eventually, "This Diamond Ring" ended up with a West Coast producer who re-worked it for *Gary Lewis and the Playboys*. When the three songwriters first heard the new single, they were less than pleased. "We were revolted," Al says. "They'd removed the soul from our R&B song and made a teenage milkshake out of it. We dismissed it on one hearing."

Others didn't. After Gary Lewis and the Playboys performed the song on The Ed Sullivan Show, it shot all the way to number one on the charts. "America had finally seen fit to recognize our talent," laughs Al. "We conveniently forgot our previous animosity toward the record and concentrated on basking in as much of the glory as we could squeeze out of it."

That was followed by another solid chart hit, "I Must Be Seeing Things," for Gene Pitney. The struggling songwriters moved up a notch or two on the industry feeding chain. Likewise, Al's individual reputation was growing as he continued getting around and making his presence known.

But the music, if not the business itself, was changing. Tin Pan Alley teenage pop was giving way to *The Beatles* and *Bob Dylan*. Dylan, in particular, had an impact on Al. "Little by little, the Dylan influences crept into my work," Al remembers. "I began fooling around composing songs on my own—blatant Dylan rip-offs. I was writing bubble gum songs by day, working in bar bands by night, and trying to squeeze every possible alternative into the time between."

One of those alternatives was an out-and-out alter ego. Al picked up a regular folk club gig at a place called *The Café Interlude*. He performed under the name "Al Casey" and was even taped by *Mike Wallace and CBS News* as part of a radio documentary.

Simultaneously, Al had also been cultivating a relationship with *Tom Wilson,* Dylan's producer at *Columbia Records.* Tom liked and trusted Al enough to offer him the rarest of opportunities: an invitation to watch a Bob Dylan recording session. The key word here is "watch." Things didn't quite turn out the way either expected and it changed Al's life forever.

From the get-go, Al had different plans. "No way I was going to visit a Dylan session and just sit there," Al states. "I was committed to play on it!"

Al showed up early and attempted to plug in and pass himself off as the guitar player. He rapidly retreated to the control room when the real guy, hot-fingered *Mike Bloomfield,* showed up.

Sure now that he'd lost his chance, Al settled in to watch. Fate would soon intervene. "They weren't too far into this long song Dylan had written before it was decided that the organ player's part would be better suited to piano. The sight of an empty seat in the studio stirred my juices once again. It didn't matter that I knew next to nothing about playing the organ...In a flash I was all over Tom Wilson, telling him that I had a great organ part for the song and, please, could I have a shot at it."

Once again, Al's determination to be where he needed to be when he needed to be paid off. In reality, he had no great part ready to play and his experience on the organ was limited, but he more than made up for his shortcomings with desire and passion.

Al walked into the studio, nervously sat down at the Hammond B-3, and created the unforgettable organ riffs on Dylan's soon-to-be-classic "Like A Rolling Stone."

His playing on that song—-and the other work he did on Dylan's *Highway 61 Revisited* album—-vaulted Al Kooper to the A-list and set him on track for his stellar career. He was all of 21 years old.

From founding Blood, Sweat & Tears, to discovering Lynyrd Skynyrd, to playing with his new group, *The Rekooperators,* Al has remained on the scene for the better part of four decades now, and he'll doubtlessly remain there, one way or the other, well into the millennium.

While his gifts are immense, his formula for success is simple, and he's remained true to it all these years. "As I look back, I see myself at 16 as someone who had 10-percent talent and 90-percent ambition," Al reflects. "Now, I see myself with the equation completely reversed."

It's said you make your own luck. And if Al is a good example of that, then it's done with hard work, courage, and an unstoppable belief in oneself.

If you keep that in mind—who knows? It could be your lucky day, someday soon.

Review this page to develop the "Al Kooper style."*
To understand Al Kooper's left-hand keyboard style, first play the 7th chords below.
Review each chord voiced with its 3rd and 7th intervals.

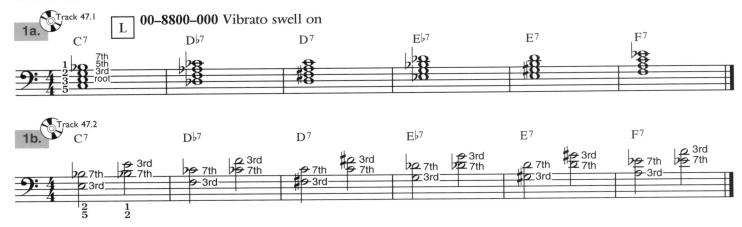

"This LH, playing the 3rd and 7th intervals of a chord, was a real breakthrough for me. It changed my life. It is totally not rootsie."—A.K.

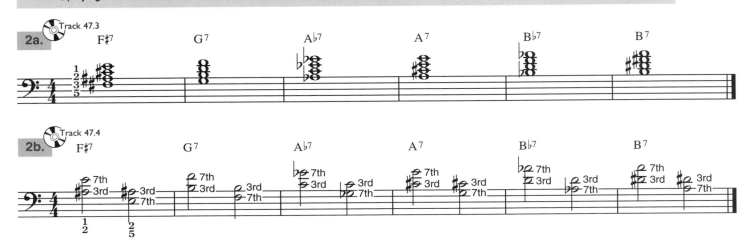

Much of Al's chordal movement is chromatic, by half step.
To better understand this style, play and memorize these chromatic scale exercises.

*To match the CDs B-3 sounds, add the following to both manuals:
 • select the B♮ preset
 • use the second set of drawbars

Licks in the Style of Al Kooper

Al uses this setting ⓤ 00–8800–000 and Ⓛ 00–8800–000, (both manuals), during most of his playing.

Track 48.1

4a.

"My favorite blues key is F. I'm born and raised in F. To play Al Kooper, you need to play the F blues scale fast."—A.K.

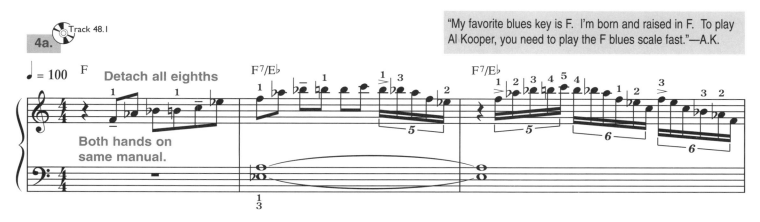

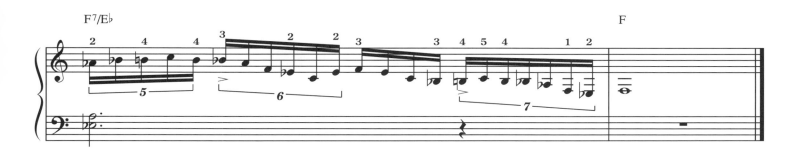

Track 48.2

4b.

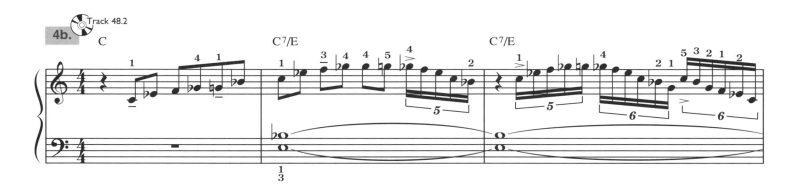

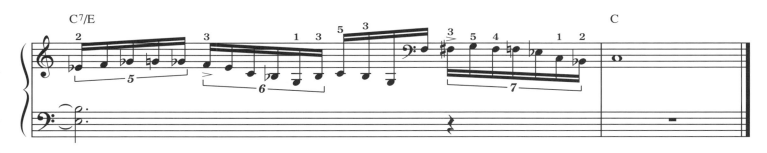

Transpose to B♭ and then combine to play the 12-bar blues.

"When my LH plays, I vary the level, however the 3rd and 4th drawbars are always equal."—A.K.

example: L   00–5500–000

Al often combines two different blues scales in his improv. Here, Al combines C and A blues scales.

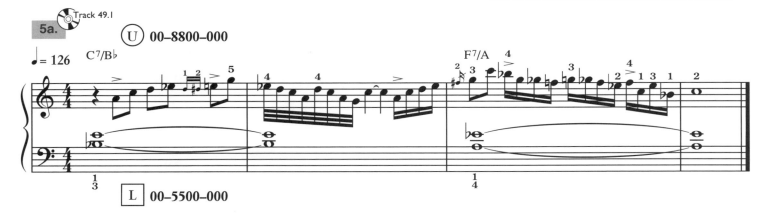

Al combines G and E blues scales here.

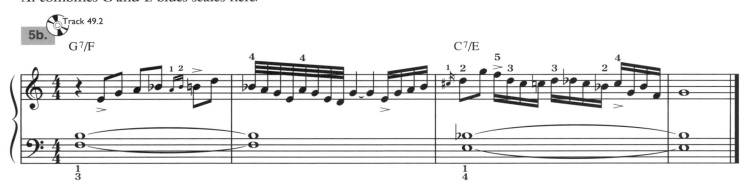

Al combines C and A blues scales here.

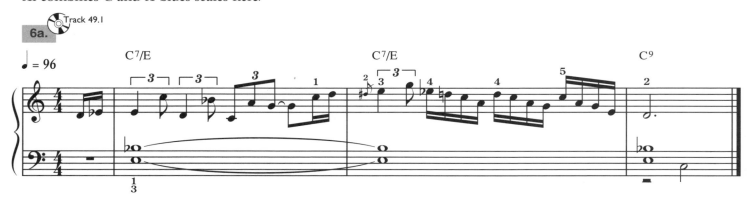

Al combines F and D blues scales here.

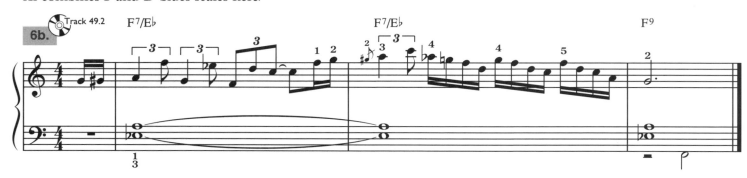

9a. Track 51.1

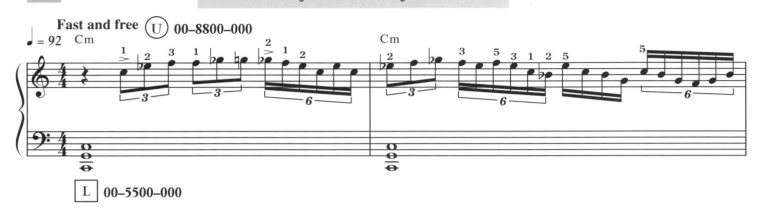

"Add tremolo during vocal solos or during 7th chords."—A.K.

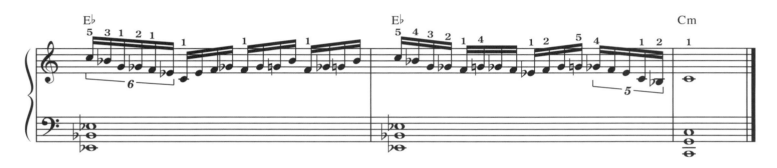

On Developing Skills . . .

"Building your ear is very important. Listening to records can't be beat. You learn to pick things up from them and assimilate the knowledge. That really sharpens your ear."—A.K.

9b. Track 51.2

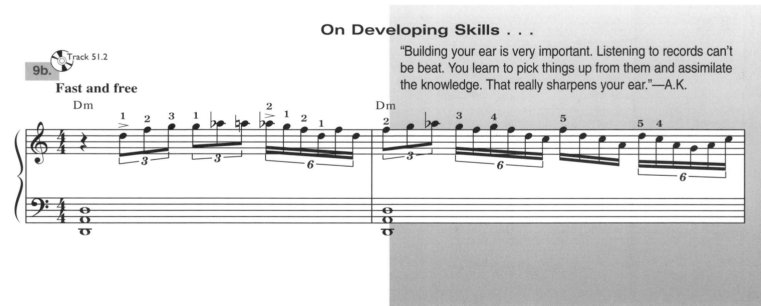

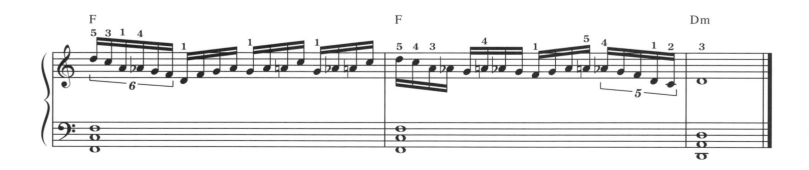

GOTHAM BLUES

Track 52

U 00–8800–000

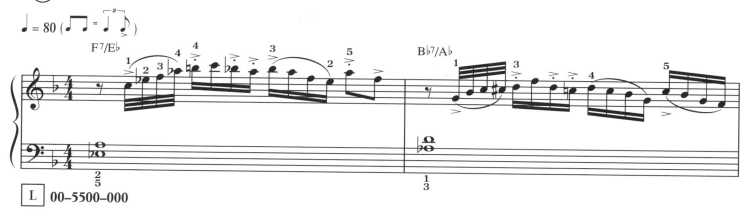

L 00–5500–000

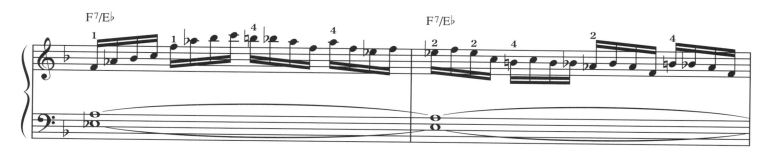

"I'm always fiddlin' around with the Leslie for different effects. Change it from slow to fast for a crescendo."—A.K.

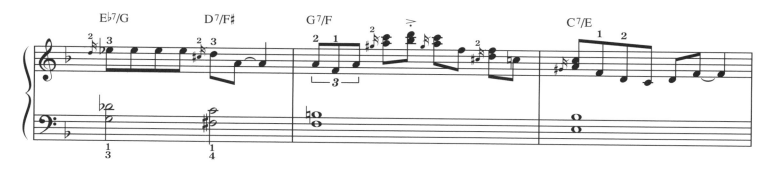

Al Kooper turnarounds.

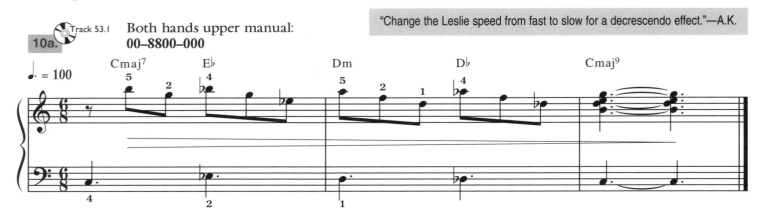

"Change the Leslie speed from fast to slow for a decrescendo effect."—A.K.

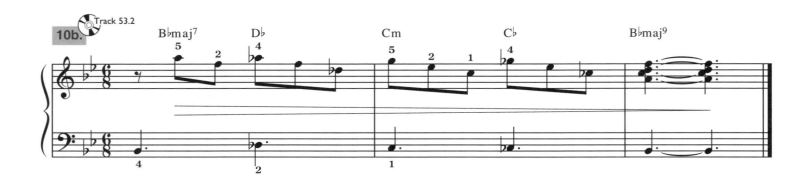

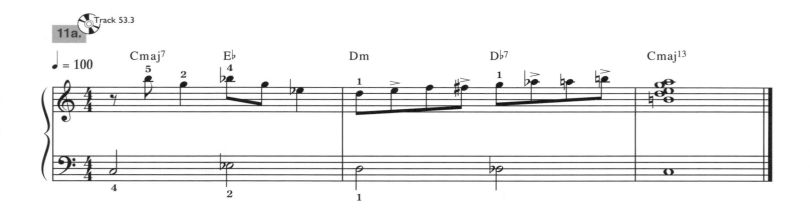

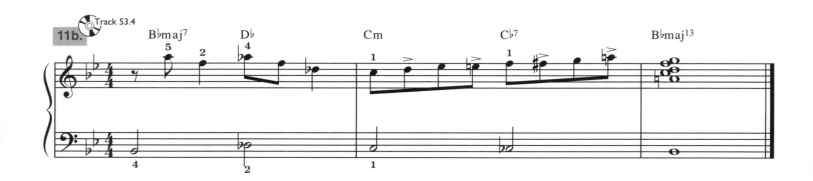

"I usually don't use percussion rockers, but you can use it for a spank sound during short repeated chords, (U) 88–8800–000 "—A.K.

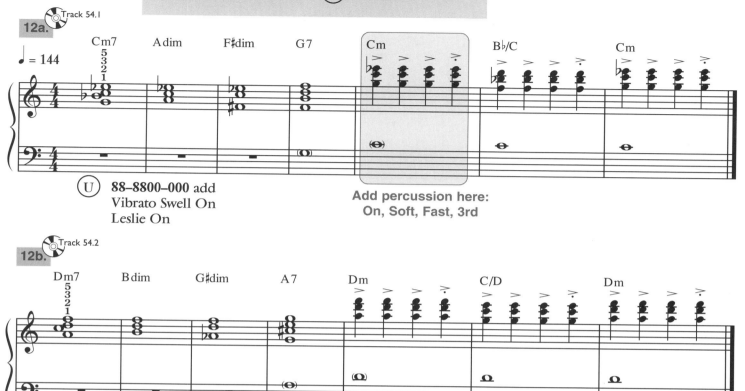

12a. Track 54.1

♩ = 144

(U) 88–8800–000 add
Vibrato Swell On
Leslie On

Add percussion here:
On, Soft, Fast, 3rd

12b. Track 54.2

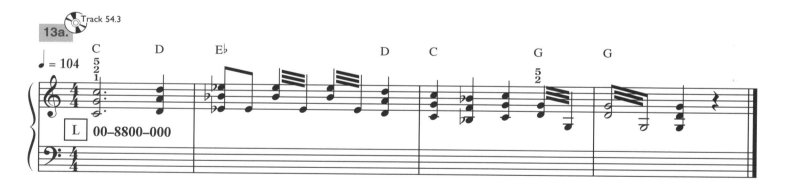

13a. Track 54.3

♩ = 104

L 00–8800–000

On Songwriting . . .

"It's different for each song. When I write a song, I usually get an urge like I'm hungry. I'll often be listening to something that I enjoy that's really creative, and I'll go to the piano and start singing. I keep doing it until something sticks. The first line is stream-of-consciousness and then it continues from there."—A.K.

13b. Track 54.4

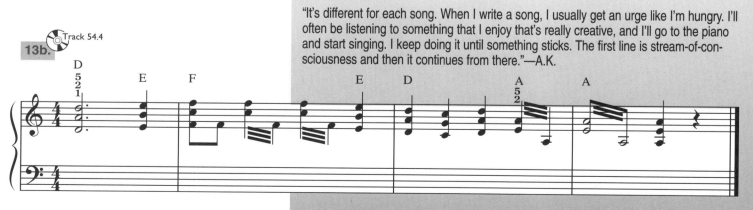

Accent the 8th notes for an authentic swing feel.

"During guitar solos, I usually move my RH up to the upper manual and setting, (U) 00–8800–000."—A.K.

BROADWAY BLUES 🎵 Track 55

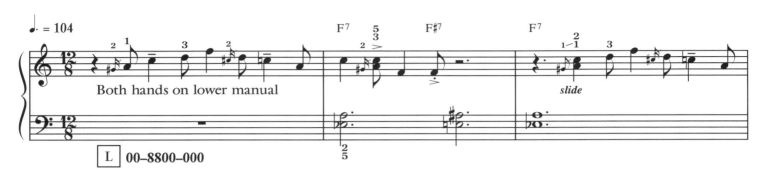

Both hands on lower manual

L 00–8800–000

LH on upper manual

On Computer Technology . . .

"It's a great tool for budding arrangers. You can try out everything. I've done a couple of films and TV series with quick deadlines, and I've become very fast."—A.K.

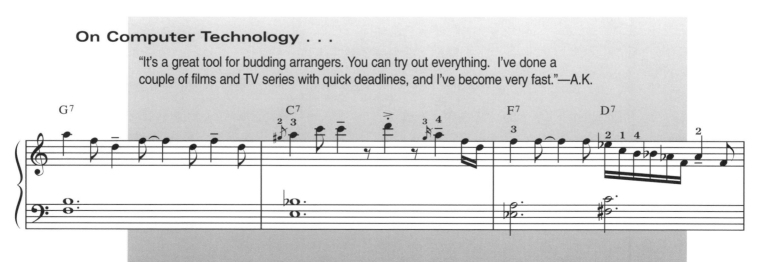

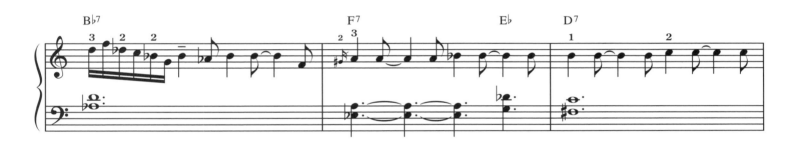

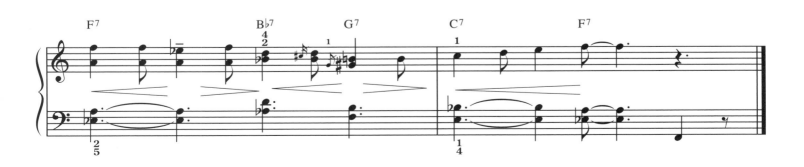

Recommended Listening — Albums

CHUCK LEAVELL

1973	Brothers and Sisters	(Allman Brothers Band)
	Laid Back	(Gregg Allman)
1974	Highway Call	(Richard Betts)
1975	Win, Lose, or Draw	(Allman Brothers Band)
1977	Sea Level	(Sea Level)
1978	On The Edge	(Sea Level)
1983	Undercover	(Rolling Stones)
1986	Dirty Work	(Rolling Stones)
1987	Hail, Hail Rock and Roll	(Chuck Berry)
1989	Steel Wheels	(Rolling Stones)
1990	Shake Your Money Maker	(Black Crowes)
1991	24 Nights	(Eric Clapton)
1992	Live In Japan	(George Harrison)
	Unplugged	(Eric Clapton)
1994	Four	(Blues Traveler)
	VooDoo Lounge	(Rolling Stones)
	Swamp Ophelia	(Indigo Girls)
1997	Bridges to Babylon	(Rolling Stones)

REESE WYNANS

1985	Soul To Soul	(Stevie Ray Vaughan and Double Trouble)
1986	Live Alive	(Stevie Ray Vaughan and Double Trouble)
1989	In Step	(Stevie Ray Vaughan and Double Trouble)
1991	The Sky Is Crying	(Stevie Ray Vaughan and Double Trouble)
1992	Love And Danger	(Joe Ely)
1996	First Blood	(Mike Henderson and The Bluebloods)
1997	Trouble Is	(Kenny Wayne Shepherd)
1998	Heavy Love Los Lonely Boys	(Buddy Guy) (Los Lonely Boys)

DR. JOHN

Gris-Gris

Dr. John's Gumbo

In The Right Place

Desitively Bonaroo

Dr. John Plays Mac Rebennack

In A Sentimental Mood

Goin' Back To New Orleans

Television

Afterglow

AL KOOPER

1965	Highway 61 Revisited	(Bob Dylan)
	Live At The Café Au Go Go	(The Blues Project)
1966	Blonde On Blonde	(Bob Dylan)
1967	Live At Town Hall	(The Blues Project)
1968	Super Session	(A. Kooper/M. Bloomfield/S. Stills)
	Child Is Father To The Man	(Blood, Sweat & Tears)
	I Stand Alone	(A. Kooper)
1969	Kooper Sessions	(A. Kooper/S. Otis)
	The Live Adventures of Mike Bloomfield & Al Kooper	
1970	Easy Does It	(A. Kooper)
1973	Pronounced Leh-nerd Skin-erd	(Lynyrd Skynyrd)
	Second Helping	(Lynyrd Skynyrd)
1975	Al's Big Deal	(A. Kooper)
	The Tubes	(The Tubes)
1980	Somewhere In England	(George Harrison)
1982	Championship Wrestling	(A. Kooper)
1985	Biograph	(Bob Dylan)
1991	Trisha Yearwood	(Trisha Yearwood)
1994	Rekooperation	(Al Kooper)
	Soul Of A Man	(Al Kooper)
1995	Playback	(Tom Petty & The Heartbreakers)
1998	I Can't Complain	(Phoebe Snow)

Bibliography and On-Line Resources

CHUCK LEAVELL
The Alabama Music Hall of Fame
http://alamhof.org

The Allman Brothers Band & Chuck Leavell
http://www.allmanbrothersband.com

Charlane Plantation & Chuck Leavell
http://www.charlane.com

REESE WYNANS
Stevie Ray Vaughan & Double Trouble
http://www.SRVDoubleTrouble.com

Texas Flood Mailing List - Stevie Ray Vaughan FAQ
http://www.smartlink.net/~jackklos/srvfaq.htm

Jerry Jeff Walker
http://www.jerryjeff.com

DR. JOHN
Under a Hoodoo Moon: The Life of the Night Tripper
by Dr. John (Mac Rebennack) with Jack Rummel
St. Martin's Griffin, 1995

The Big Book of Blues
by Robert Santelli
Penguin Books, 1993

Night-Tripping with the Good Doctor
by Tom Piazza
The New York Times, May 22, 1994

A Trip into the 'Woodshed' with Dr. John
by Mike Zwerin
The International Herald Tribune, May 19, 1994

Dr. John Gives New Orleans' Lovers Their Fix
by Dave Becker
The Oakland Tribune, March 18, 1994

Dr. John Still Does It All and Writes About It All!
by Phillip Elwood
The San Francisco Examiner, March 17, 1994

Dr. John Gets People Groovin'
by Bill Pahnelas
The Richmond Times-Dispatch, June 15, 1992

Blues on Stage Web Site
http://www.mnblues.com

The Blue Flame Café: Encyclopedia of the Blues
http://www.blueflamecafe.com/Dr_John.html

Dr. John's Place — Great New Orleans Music at Its Best
http://www.drjohn.com

iMusic Contemporary Showcase: Dr. John
http://imusic.com/showcase/contemporary/drjohn.html

The Rough Guide to Rock: Dr. John
http://www-2.roughguides.com

AL KOOPER
Backstage Passes & Backstabbing Bastards: Memoirs of a Rock 'n' Roll Survivor
by Al Kooper
Billboard Books, 1998

Al Kooper Official Web Site
http://www.alkooper.com

HAMMOND B-3 ORGAN
History of the Hammond B-3 Organ
http://theatreorgans.com/hammond/index.html

About the Authors

KAREN ANN KRIEGER

Karen Ann Krieger is building an international reputation as a pianist, lecturer/clinician and teacher.

An accomplished classical and jazz pianist, Ms. Krieger is equally at home writing piano compositions or working in a recording studio with the latest computer synthesizer technology.

Under the direction of Columbia and Allied Artists Management, Ms. Krieger has performed nationwide as one-half of the Neal Ramsay Duo. As a solo artist, she has also toured England, Scotland, Cyprus, and British Columbia. She has thrilled a wide range of audiences during piano and accordion performances with the Nashville Symphony, the Atlanta Russian Orchestra, and the Gregg Allman Band.

Ms. Krieger holds an M.M. in Piano Performance from the University of Illinois. She's currently an Assistant Professor of Piano at Vanderbilt University's Blair School of Music in Nashville, Tennessee.

Ms. Krieger has also gained recognition as an ADDY award-winning television news and weather anchor. She considers covering Presidents Reagan and Carter (for whom she performed) to be her most memorable experiences.

STEPHAN FOUST

Stephan Foust is an Emmy-nominated video producer, writer and journalist, based in Nashville, Tennessee.

A former teacher and coach, Mr. Foust has won numerous Associated Press and United Press International Awards for his work in television news, plus national and international recognition for his video productions.

During his career, Mr. Foust has covered and worked with world leaders, sports stars, noted musicians and famous entertainers, but he considers marrying Karen Ann Krieger the highlight of his life.

Blues Scales and Fingerings